Christopher Markert

Seeing Well Again Without Your Glasses

Christopher Markert

Seeing Well Again Without Your Glasses

The C. W. Daniel Company Ltd
Saffron Walden

First published in Great Britain by
The C. W. Daniel Company Limited
1 Church Path, Saffron Walden, Essex
CB10 1JP, England

ISBN 0 85207 151 5

Set in 11/12pt Photina by White Crescent Press Ltd, Crescent Road, Luton, Beds
and printed and bound by Mansell Ltd, Industrial Estate East, Freebournes Road,
Witham, Essex.

Contents

Part One

Seeing Well Means Being Well

What this Book Does for You

Like everyone else you want to enjoy good health, vitality and general well-being. You want your life to be bright and colourful, and you want to think and see clearly. You also want to look healthy.

These are the very qualities we admire in young children. But as we grow up we seem to gradually lose them. This process can start quite early, and you may have noticed some symptoms in yourself. Do you still feel full of life most of the time, do you enjoy most days, is your body still flexible, and do you see as well as you used to?

It has been found that most young men today are physically or mentally so inadequate that they could not pass the admission test of the armed forces even if they wanted to. Only three generations ago most men in this age group were found to be in prime condition. Statistics show that about twenty percent of the children entering school today have faulty vision. But by the time they leave school the percentage has risen to eighty. Is it 'normal' to have blurred vision at the age of 18? Primitive people living under natural conditions are known for their keen eyesight, and most of them enjoy perfect vision into old age. Heart attack and hardening of the arteries used to be a disease of old people. Now it is found even among teenagers.

These are only a few examples among many. They serve as warning signals. They tell us that something is wrong with our present way of life and our attitude towards health.

But an alternative does exist, and many people have already discovered it. Others have never lost the secret. Anybody who really wishes to improve his/her condition can do so. All it takes is the right information and know-how. This book contains a practical package of knowledge that is easy to understand and to apply. With it you can improve your eyesight. You can also enhance your ability to think clearly, and to enjoy greater health and well-being. Furthermore, you can change all aspects of your life for the better and open the door to a brighter future.

This may sound like a tall statement. But by the time you have finished the book and followed the simple instructions, you will take the benefits for granted. You will then probably say to yourself 'I wish I had come across this information sooner'.

Here are some of the benefits that you can derive from this method:

You find it easier to relax mentally and physically, and to cope with the stresses of daily life. Instead of worrying about the future and the past, you make the best of the present. Your life comes into focus and you see your way through confusing situations. Your memory and your ability to picture things in your mind improve.

Rigid attitudes, preconceived ideas and subconscious hang-ups begin to drop away as you learn to let the mind/body function more joyfully and efficiently. If your vision is faulty, you gradually decrease your dependence on cumbersome glasses or lenses. In many cases the need for them disappears entirely. If your vision is now adequate, you can decrease the chances that you will need glasses or lenses in the future.

Headaches, other aches and conditions tend to occur less often or disappear. As your mind becomes balanced, your posture improves, you move about with more poise. You breathe more evenly and deeply. You begin to sense which foods are best for you, and which substances harm your well-being and vision. You understand your body and its ability to heal itself, and you rely less on medicines, gadgets or operations that may have harmful side-effects. You also find it easier to control over-weight.

You discover that the eyes are reliable indicators of inner states and the state of your health, and that they can guide you in many ways. This awareness also helps you read other people's condition from their eyes.

Finally, you achieve more in your daily life, while at the

10

same time you do things with less effort. Through your ability to see and perceive better, you become less accident-prone. You are more in control of your life and you no longer blame circumstances or others for your own habits or mistakes. Your inner harmony radiates and brightens your relations with the people around you. People feel more attracted to you, and you feel more at ease with them.

But Does it Really Work?

Naturally you will have your doubts about any unfamiliar method. Here are some questions people have asked, and the answers:

Q. If my vision is normal, why should I bother to read this book?

A. Normal eyesight is not yet perfect. You can still gain all the benefits of perfect vision listed on the previous pages.

Q. Why should I start a time-consuming programme when I can get good vision by buying a pair of glasses?

A. The programme is hardly time-consuming once you got it going, and the benefits far outweigh the inconvenience. Furthermore, glasses do not improve your eyes. In fact, they weaken the eyes, as will be explained later. Glasses are also inconvenient, cumbersome and expensive, especially because in most cases they have to be replaced periodically by stronger ones.

Q. It's in our family. How can I have perfect vision if my parents and grandparents all wear glasses?

A. You can improve your vision even if you inherit a certain pre-disposition. But many people are uninformed in this respect or they have a mental block. They think they know it all. Don't let such negative opinions influence you.

Q. At my age it's too late. Everyone knows that the eyesight begins to fail with advancing age. Why fight the inevitable?

A. Any organ that isn't used properly begins to atrophy or malfunction. If you stay in bed for only a few days, your muscles begin to deteriorate and your joints stiffen. If you don't use your mind, it gets lazy and foggy. The same is true of the eyes. Some people stay physically fit up to the age of one hundred, while others give

12

up and allow their organs to deteriorate.

Q. It may work for others, but the eye specialist told me that nothing can be done in my case.

A. Perhaps the specialist cannot do anything, but you can. The body has uncanny healing powers that work for the person who really wants to be healed and who does something about it. If you are strongly motivated to become whole again, and have faith in the regenerating powers of your organism, you can literally work wonders. Most doctors know this, but they have little control over a patient's faith and motivation, or else they have no time to explain psycho-somatic connections. Hippocrates, the founder of medical science, said: 'The doctor can treat a disease, but Nature heals.'

Q. If I stopped wearing glasses now, wouldn't this hurt my eyes?

A. Glasses and contact lenses are like crutches. They enable weak eyes to see, but they weaken them still further, instead of strengthening them. If you gradually begin to see better without them, your eyes learn to function better, as explained in later chapters.

Q. I heard about another eye-improvement method that didn't seem to help much. How does this method described here differ?

A. It is simpler, more fun and more down-to-earth. Therefore people are more likely to put it into practice and to get the benefits. The book is also more comprehensive and explains many benefits not mentioned in previous works.

Q. Is there any scientific proof that the method works?

A. The method was pioneered in the 1920's by Dr W. H. Bates, the famous New York ophthalmologist. Since then others have added to it, and hundreds of thousands of people have improved their eyesight and wellbeing through it. Aldous Huxley was cured from nearblindness by the Bates Method, and he wrote a book about his experience.

Q. What about those conditions that are absolutely incurable?

A. Even then the information in this book helps to understand and ameliorate the condition, or to retard the disease. But thousands of cases that had been declared hopeless by the experts have been partly or wholly cured through the methods described here.

Many of these 'miracle cures' have been documented; and anyone who understands the Bates Method will find these stories quite logical and natural.

Q. Where can I get additional information about all this?
A. The bibliography at the end of the book lists literature and the addresses of professional organisations. Personal tuition by a competent and trained vision instructor is usually preferable to written instructions, but it may not be available in your area, or you may not be able to spare the time and/or money for travel and lectures.
Q. How much time is necessary for the daily exercises?
A. This depends on you and your circumstances. You can do much for your eyes by merely adopting certain habits in your daily life, without exercising. But if your visual problem is urgent, you will want to get into these habits faster by setting aside time for daily training sessions. Even very busy readers should try each exercise at least once, to get the feel of it.

Test Your EYE-Q

At this point you will want to know your present ability to see, so that you can later measure your progress. To determine you EYE-Quotient is quite easy, and it works somewhat like the well-known Intelligence Quotient (IQ). Both tests use a scale from 0–200, and average ability lies in the middle between these two extremes, at 100.

An EYE-Q of 200 would thus stand for perfect vision, an EYE-Q of 100 for average vision, and an EYE-Q of 50 for poor vision.

To establish your EYE-Q, simply read the EYE-Q Chart on pages 18 and 19, under good lighting conditions (without glasses or lenses). Follow the lines down until you can read no further, first from a distance of 1 ft (30cm) and then from 20 ft. (6m). Numbers in the margin next to the last line you can read indicate your EYE-Q, left numbers for near vision and right numbers for far vision. If you can see well at a distance of 20 ft (6 m) you can also see well at the far distance or at the horizon.

Enter these numbers in the EYE-Q Progress Chart in the back of the book, so that you can keep track of periodic changes and improvements. You will find that your EYE-Q changes more often than you had thought. In fact, your vision fluctuates constantly. Don't get discouraged, therefore, if you see less clearly at certain times. Improvement will take the form of a long-term trend, although there have been many cases of instant change through this method.

Normal Vision
(according to Snellen Test Card used by opticians)

Size of type you can read without glasses at various distances:

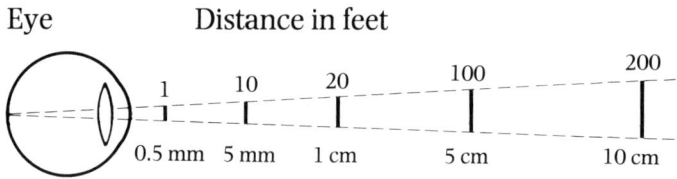

Eye   Distance in feet

1   10   20   100   200

0.5 mm   5 mm   1 cm   5 cm   10 cm

EYE-Q Chart

Read the chart under good lighting conditions, without glasses, as far down the lines as you can. First read from a distance of 1 ft. (30 cm) and then from a distance of 20 ft. (6 m).

The number in the margin next to the last line you can read is your present EYE-Q. Numbers in the left margin measure your NEAR EYE-Q, while numbers in the right margin measure your FAR EYE-Q.

YOU

FIND IT

EASIER TO REL

MENTALLY AND PHYSIC [100]

AND TO COPE WITH THE STRE 150

OF DAILY LIFE. INSTEAD OF WORRYING AB 200

THE FUTURE AND THE PAST, YOU MAKE THE BEST OF THE PRESENT. YOUR LIFE CO 400

INTO FOCUS AND YOU SEE YOUR WAY THROUGH CONFUSING SITUATIONS. YOUR MEMORY AND YOUR ABILITY TO PICTURE THINGS IN YOUR 700

MIND IMPROVE. RIGID ATTITUDES, PRECONCEIVED IDEAS AND UNCONSCIOUS HANG-UPS BEGIN TO DROP AWAY AS YOU LEARN TO LET THE MIND/BODY FUNCTION MORE JOYFULLY AND EFFICIENTLY. IF YOUR VISIO 1000

IS FAULTY, YOU GRADUALLY DECREASE YOUR DEPENDENCE ON CUMBERSOME GLASSES OR LENSES IN MANY CASES THE NEED FOR THEM DISAPPEARS ENTIRELY IF YOUR VISION IS NOW ADEQUATE, YOU CAN DECREASE THE CHANCES THAT YOU WILL NEED GLASSES OR LENSE 1500

IN THE FUTURE. HEADACHES, OTHER ACHES AND CONDITIONS TEND TO OCCUR LESS OFTEN OR DISAPPEAR. AS YOUR MIND BECOMES BALANCED, YOUR POSTURE IMPROVES. YOUR POSTURE IMPROVES, YOU MOVE ABOUT WITH MORE POISE. YOU BREATHE MORE EVENLY AND DEEPLY. YOU BEGIN TO SENSE WHICH FOODS ARE BEST FOR YOU AND WHICH SUBSTANCES HARM YOUR WELL-BEING AND VISIO 2000

5

7,5

10

20

35

50

75

[100]

The Many Causes of Imperfect Vision

Why do some people enjoy a high level of well-being while others seem to fall from one illness or misery into another? Are they just unlucky, are they forced to live under unfavourable conditions, or did they inherit a poor constitution?

It would be unfair to blame someone for getting the 'flu', an ulcer or cancer. To prevent any single disease of this type can be difficult or impossible. But people are undoubtedly responsible for their general condition to a great extent, which in turn is the result of their living habits. Improper habits lower the resistance of the organism and open the door to all kinds of maladies, including poor vision. Not all poor vision is caused by faulty habits, of course, but habits are a contributing factor.

We don't like to be told that we are to blame for our unsatisfactory condition. We find it much easier to blame an external cause. Then we can hire an expert to eradicate the evil with chemicals (medicines), gadgets (braces, crutches, glasses) or by cutting off the affected parts (surgery). The expert is sometimes aware of the real cause. But he/she also knows that most patients would resent any hints in this direction, and that they would resist his attempts to make them change their way of life.

Some old-style family doctors did have the time, the long-term contact with their patients and the desire to see the whole picture and treat the whole person. But modern specialists tend to see the affected organ only. They are paid to make the symptom disappear, and they usually make a good job of it. When the general weakness of the organism causes other symptoms later, this is not seen as anybody's fault.

Perhaps the most serious indictment of their methods can be seen in the fact that their own health is no better than that of the population as a whole, and according to some statistics it is worse . Although they do their best to heal their patients (and themselves), they are overwhelmed by such a flood of technical data and new discoveries that they tend to lose sight of the basic laws of healing. This is a problem we all face to a greater or lesser extent in our current age of swift technological progress and specialization.

Many doctors are aware of this, and Laurence Krantz, MD commented recently in *Healing Currents*:

"Relative to this question of true education for the healers, I realize it takes a lot of courage for many people who are health care professionals, who have been through many years of training and have degrees after their names and great respect in their communities, to actually admit they need further training to begin to be effective healers. . . . I very much appreciate the openess and courageous attitude exemplified by many health professionals who are willing to move beyond their traditional training and say, in effect, 'These techniques are fine in handling certain external situations but I need to go back to elementary school as far as discovering a true relationship with life and the laws of healing is concerned, if I am really going to be effective in my service'."[1]

In ancient China, doctors were often hired to prevent disease. They were paid a certain monthly fee for keeping the client in top condition and to nip any advancing illness in the bud. If the client did get ill, the fee was discontinued until health was restored, and the doctor had to pay for all medicines and treatments out of his own pocket. Today we are justly proud of our modern medical technology, but we have not yet developed an effective scheme of preventive medicine. Many attempts are being made to fill this need, and the book you are reading now is one of them.

The word 'vision' has two meanings. Firstly, it refers to the ability to see in a strictly optical sense. Secondly, it implies the ability of the mind to see ahead, to perceive future developments and to act accordingly. Ancient scriptures speak of the see'ers or 'men of vision', the leaders and prophets who know the right path, who follow the cosmic laws and point the way for others. When it comes to our modern concept of health, it seems that our vision is as poor as our eyesight. Our methods are in many ways short-sighted, they do not harmonize with life and the laws of Nature.

Our attitude toward the eyes is a good example. We tend to think of them as more or less isolated organs that are attached to the forehead for our convenience and that slowly wear out, much like teeth. But the eyes are in fact delicate parts of a complex body, which in turn lives in a complex environment. Any imbalance of the mind, body or environment can affect the vision. An imbalance is especially harmful if it becomes habitual or permanent, when parts of the eyes can lose their flexibility, mobility or transparency.

The following list of disorders covers mostly the more common optical defects. Rare and serious diseases are discussed in later chapters.

The main causes of poor vision can be divided into mental, physical and environmental ones, although they all overlap. Dr Bates described the mental factors as the main culprits, although they may in turn have underlying causes of a physical or environental nature. The mental habit of straining to see, for example, may partly be caused by drinking too much alcohol (physical) or by exposure to excessive noise (environmental).

A.   Mental Factors

When your eyes do not see clearly for one reason or another, you may be tempted to 'make them see'. You force the eyes, you strain to see. But the eyes are such delicate organisms that any conscious interference only confuses them. They function best when they are at ease, when they can adjust by themselves, unconsciously, automatically. You can always assume that your eyes work as well as possible under existing circumstances. They tend to focus automatically and sharply on any object that truly interests and concerns you.

One of the best ways to make your vision blur is to look at an object that bores you. From your own experience you know that you can read through an entire novel in one stretch without any effort of the eyes whatsoever, – if the novel is interesting. But if you are forced to read a boring or irrelevant book, your vision tires and blurs on the first page. School children are forced for years to read material that seems boring and irrelevant to them, and this is probably the main reason why most of them develop poor vision. (See also The Eyesight of Children page 50).

But lack of interest is not always the reason. Sometimes you look at something that really concerns you, and you still cannot see it clearly. The reason then may be your habit of hurrying through life, of not letting the mind and the eyes take their time to adjust and to focus. The eyes often need several minutes to get used to certain conditions.

Another reason may be your over-anxious attempts to do well or to avoid mistakes.

If you reject certain unpleasant aspects of your life, if you tend to close your mind toward unpleasant facts, your eyes will be less eager to see, and they will try to find ways of malfunctioning. A realistic and constructive mental attitude, on the other hand, encourages the eyes to function optimally.

Your inner balance may be disturbed through tension, stress, grief, anxiety, worry or fear. You may be harbouring negative emotions like hate, anger, greed or envy.

Are you perhaps in the habit of over-extending yourself by getting into debt or taking on too many obligations, and then worrying about the consequences?

Or do you sometimes refuse to admit that you are tired and need to rest first? Are you in other ways working against your nature or suppressing bodily functions? The eyes are a link between body and mind, and any inner stress interferes with their function.

Does your life presently lack focus, or is it revolving around irrelevant goals? Is your attitude toward life somewhat depressive or destructive, do you feel that life is meaningless or that the cosmic order is senseless? If your mind is habitually out of focus, so are your eyes.*

B. Physical Factors

The condition of your eyes can only be as good as the condition of the body of which they are part. Just as any other part of the body, the eyes need a continuous supply of nutrients and oxygen through the blood stream. They also need sunlight, exercise and periodic rest.

This means, for instance, that you see best when you are in the habit of eating the right foods and of avoiding harmful substances. By being aware of your eyes in the coming weeks and months, you will begin to sense which of your habits contribute to good vision and which do not. You will soon realise your tolerance level for alcohol, tobacco, drugs or medicine.

Lacking exercise and poor breathing habits inhibit your blood circulation, and this also affects your eyes. Poor posture or an S-shaped spine diminish chest volume and breathing. A rigid body and stiff joints lessen the mobility of your mind and eyes, and are often the first signs of advancing illness.

Your vision can suffer from the habit of staring at fixed objects for long periods, without moving the eyes, eyelids, the head or the neck. This often happens during routine work, while watching television, or when driving on motorways.

The habit of staying up late by artificial light is not conducive to good health or good vision. The same goes for irregular schedules that upset inner biological clocks, as in night shifts, alternating shifts, and intercontinental flights (jet lag).

Some of these conditions may be unavoidable. Bakers, for instance, have to work at night, and airline crew have to make intercontinental flights. But by being aware of

---

*See also *Let Yourself Grow* by the same author (Wildwood House Ltd, London, 1978), published in the USA as *Your Hidden Potential* (Newcastle Publishing Company, Van Nugs, CA, 1980).

these influences, and by trying to compensate for them, the negative effects can usually be minimized.

Any illness, from the common cold to a broken leg, will tend to upset the delicate balance in your eyes. Especially virus diseases like influenza can throw your mind and vision temporarily out of focus.

C. Environmental Factors

In recent years the word 'ecology' has become fashionable, simply because the quality of our environment has deteriorated so much. There are still plenty of beautiful and unspoilt spaces left in the world, but most people insist on crowding into monstrous cities. Even the ones who still live in rural areas have become part of the machine age and the television era to a great extent.

Our ancestors who lived in the country two hundred years ago had their problems, but we certainly have ours. Although we enjoy many advantages of modern civilization, we also have to put up with its many influences that are detrimental to our bodies, minds, nerves and eyes.

We have to endure air pollution from exhaust gases, smog and industrial fumes. Our food is often contaminated by artificial preservatives, colouring, pesticides, hormones, etc. Our nerves get frazzled by noise pollution from traffic, airplanes, machinery, loudspeakers, television sets, transistor radios, etc. We get brainwashed by the incessant pressure from the mass media that are forever trying to sell us things or ideas. All can contribute to the mental and visual strain of civilized life.

Much of the time we also have to put up with overcrowded conditions and an overly civilized way of life that deprives us of the stimulating contact with the elements. We see mainly man-made scenes and seldom encounter natural landscapes which offer rest and variety to the eyes. Natural sunlight unfiltered by glass windows has become a rarity in the lives of many. Long exposure to neon light has proven to be harmful to the eyes and the nervous system.

Quite aside from these man-made factors, your eyesight

can be temporarily affected by changing weather conditions, low pressure fronts, rainy weather, extreme heat or cold, humidity or dryness – and by unfavourable lighting conditions.

How Your Eyes Function

You communicate with your environment through the five senses of sight, hearing, taste, touch and smell. Your sense of sight is by far the most important of these, and it is also the most complex. It is one of the great miracles of creation, and the technical particulars are almost beyond human comprehension.

The light-sensitive layer inside the eye, the retina, consists of 100,000,000 rods for seeing black and white, and of 7,000,000 cones for seeing colour. These connect with the brain through 1,000,000 separate lines in the form of the optic nerve.[2]

The eyeball of an adult measures about one inch in diameter and is slightly inflated. It cleans and lubricates itself through tears which contain a strong germicide. It is mobile in its socket, and six muscles attached to the outside can turn it in all directions. The lens inside the eye is also adjustable through tiny internal muscles. The pupil in front of the lens can open or close according to lighting conditions, through expansion or contraction of the surrounding iris. The pupil in the centre of the visible eye appears black because it exposes the dark interior. The iris gives the eye its colour; when it fully opens to let in a maximum amount of light, the pupil becomes 17 times as large in area as in the contracted state.[3]

During darkness the retina becomes 25,000 times as sensitive as in daylight, and it is a thousand times more sensitive than the most sensitive high-speed film.

The three pairs of muscles that direct each eye are hardly ever at rest during waking hours, and healthy eyes move continuously back and forth and up and down in a scanning motion. They move even at night during the dream state. An incredible feat of co-ordination is required to move both eyes in unison in the desired direction, and any imbalance results in squint or other disorders. The muscles function automatically and unconsiously to a great extent, but at the same time we can direct the eyes consciously in any direction we wish. This is so because the muscles are partly striped (consciously controlled) and partly smooth (unconsiously controlled). This dual personality is their great advantage, but it also makes them vulnerable to nervous and mental disorders.

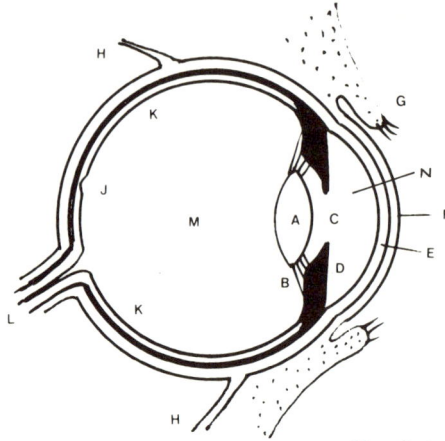

A	Lens	H	Outer Muscle
B	Ciliary Muscles	J	Fovea Centralis
C	Pupil	K	Retina
D	Iris	L	Optic Nerve
E	Cornea	M	Vitreous Body
F	Conjunctiva	N	Aqueous Liquid
G	Eyelid and lashes		

The eye functions in many ways like a camera: light enters through a lens in front and is focused on a light-sensitive layer in the back. But the focusing in a camera is done by moving the lens back and forth, while in the eye the lens can change its shape through tiny internal (ciliary) muscles. When the muscles contract, the lens is adjusted for close vision. When the muscles are at rest, the eye focuses on distant objects.

According to Bates, the eye can also learn to accomodate to distance by changing its shape and focal length. This controversial theory would explain why some people with hardened lenses can accomodate very well. The argument about this theory is still raging, but the fact is that the Bates Method works in practice.

The larger the pupil opens, the more critical becomes the focusing. When the pupil contracts to the size of a pinhead, the range of a clear vision increases. This phenomenon is known by photographers as 'depth of field'. Such knowledge is useful for all people with defective vision because it tells them they can see more sharply under good lighting conditions when their pupils are smallest.

The following experiment will help you understand how your eyes function. Look at the capital T at the beginning of the last sentence, and don't move your eyes while you count to ten. Did you see the T better and better by looking at it for a long time? No, on the contrary, the image got weaker. Now look at the letter again, but let your eyes scan back and forth, up and down and across it. The letter is coming into sharper focus. Later chapters will explain more fully why you see best when your eyes are mobile and when you avoid staring.

Are you right-eyed or left-eyed? One of your eyes is dominant. To find out, stetch out one arm and look at an object through a circle formed by your thumb and index finger. Now close first the right eye and then the left. Your dominant eye is the one that still sees the object through the circle. Right-eyed people tend to be more rational and logical, while left-eyed people are more guided by imagination, and intuition.

Another curious phenomenon is the 'blind spot' in your field of vision, which results from a blank area in the retina where the optic nerve enters. To find it, close one eye and look at a small coin held at arm's length. Now focus on a more distant object located just behind the coin, for example a spot on the wall. Then slowly move the coin out sideways. It will disappear from your vision at one point (the blind spot) and re-appear further out.

The inside of the eye seems black when seen through the pupil, but the retina covering the back of the inner eye is actually orange-red. To see this colour in someone's eyes is quite an experience, but you need a retinoscope, opthalmoscope or a similar instrument for this.

What Your Eyes Reveal

The eyes are more revealing than any other part of the body. In a conversation, we watch the eyes for additional clues. A raised eyebrow or a frown speak for themselves. We 'give someone the eye', a 'stolen look' or a 'sideways glance'. We 'look through someone' or give someone 'a blank stare'. We seek eye contact if we are interested, or we avoid it when we are not. Our eyes can belie or confirm anything we say. Often we can get through to a person or a group through eye communication when words fail. Just by looking at a person's eyes we can often see his/her state of mind in a fraction of a second. As Ralph Waldo Emerson said: 'The eyes of men converse as much as their tongues, with the advantage that the ocular dialect needs no dictionary, but is understood the world over.'

Children and animals read eyes instinctively, they can sense whether a person is friendly or hostile, happy or down-cast, tense or relaxed. Grown-ups who deal with children should keep in mind that eye contact is often more important than verbal contact, that it is in any case more immediate and direct.

Women tend to communicate better than men, not only verbally but also through eye contact. They look at the other person steadily, not only when they listen but also when they speak. Men are often so pre-occupied with what they want to say that they look away when they speak. But both sexes avoid eye contact when they are unsure of themselves, when they try to conceal something, or when they are not interested.[4]

Curiously enough, the eyes themselves do not express much, except for the colour of the iris, the size of the pupil and the movement of the eyeballs. It is the area around the eyes that makes them so revealing. You can easily prove this to yourself by covering a person's face with a sheet of paper into which two small holes of one centimetre each have been cut to let the eyes look through. The eyes you see through the holes reveal little or nothing about the person's state of mind, because the surrounding eyelids, eyebrows and other parts are not visible.

But by looking at the iris only you can actually tell a great deal about a person's health, or your own. The eyes are the only transparent organ in the body, and through them you can observe the condition of tissues and the central nervous system. With nothing more than a large magnifying glass and a flash light you can have a glimpse into the body's interior. Move to within a foot of the eyes you want to observe. Use a mirror to watch your own eyes, with the lens right on top of it.

By studying and comparing the eyes of different people in this way, you will soon discover that each iris has its own structure. Watch for variations in the shape of the inner and outer rim, and for the density and regularity of the fibres radiating between the rims. Generally speaking, a healthy person has few irregularities, perfectly circular rims and fibres of smooth, fine density. When the fibres are unevenly arranged, with knots and spaces between them, you can diagnose a lack of vitality and low resistance to illness. A deformation of the inner rim, which is actually an extension of the retina and the central nervous system, indicates a serious imbalance in the body. The pupil then appears not round but oval or dented.

The visible fibres in the iris, being part of the central nervous system, have connections to all parts of the body. They register irregularities in the body tissue and metabolism, and they can reveal a predisposition to certain disorders long before they manifest as illness. The presence of toxins or acids, and the functioning of glands can be monitored by watching the iris. An imbalance in the upper organs is ususally reflected by irregularities in the upper iris, the lower organs correspond to the lower iris, the left organs to the left side of the iris, and the right organs to the right side of the iris. To diagnose further than this would require thorough medical training but the knowledge given here enables you to observe the state of your health periodically, to correct imbalances in the body and to prevent illness in most cases. As soon as you notice irregularities in the iris, you may want to revise your diet, start a balanced exercise programme or change your living habits until the symptoms disappear. If you try to achieve the same end with medicines, the symptoms in the iris will usually not disappear, but merely shift to another area.[5]

The size of the pupil is also revealing. It expands when you want to see more for example, and contracts when you want to shut out something like bright light or an unpleasant sight. Shrewd traders can look at a buyer's pupils to see whether their offer is being accepted or rejected. Especially the pupils of light-skinned people change visibly with their emotions. As people get older, their pupils contract slightly, probably because their increasing far-sightedness makes their vision sharper when the pupils are small.[6]

Eyes also play the role of lie detectors. Dr Bates found that a person may have good vision while telling the truth, but that the vision instantly blurs when he/she says something that is not true. Even when this is done with no intent to deceive, and even if the untruth is only imagined, the eyes will immediately lose their focus. Lying apparently causes the mind to strain, and the eyes cannot properly function under strain. Even if you read the letters low down on the EYE-Q Chart, and you intentionally misread one letter, you lose your focus for a moment. If someone else states that you are twenty-five years old when your actual age is twenty-seven, observation with a retinoscope would indicate a sudden error of refraction. As soon as you reply that you are really twenty-seven years old, your vision becomes normal again. But if you then imagine that you are older or younger, the vision would blur once again.

One other thing that the skin around the eyes reveals is habitual tension. Wrinkles and crow's feet are caused by the habit of 'screwing' the eyes, a sure sign of mental strain. This is common in people with poor vision, who find sunlight irritating and who tend to stretch the head forward. People with perfect vision, on the other hand, have relaxed eyes, and the skin around the eyes remains quite smooth even into old age.

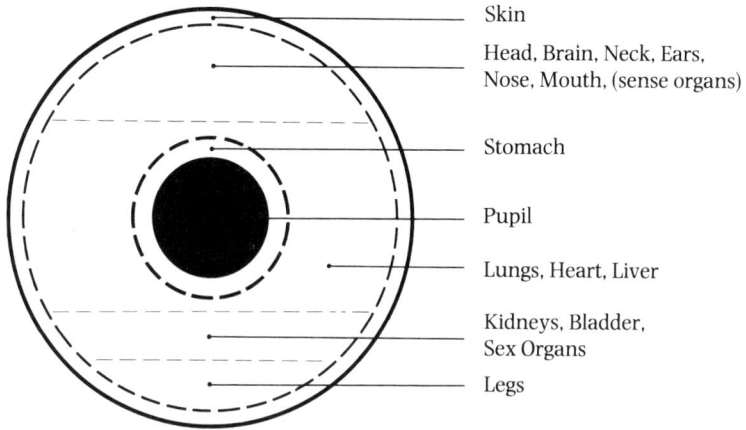

Skin

Head, Brain, Neck, Ears, Nose, Mouth, (sense organs)

Stomach

Pupil

Lungs, Heart, Liver

Kidneys, Bladder, Sex Organs

Legs

Basic Iridology Chart

Visual Defects

This chapter provides a short summary of the more common disorders. A detailed description with suggestions on how to deal with them follows in Part III.

Poor vision takes the form of short-sightedness or far-sightedness in nine cases out of ten, sometimes accompanied by a distortion in the lens or cornea called astigmatism. These are called 'errors of refraction' or 'optical defects'. They make us see things in a blurred or distorted way, because the light rays entering the eye are not properly focused on the retina. Some text books list eye-strain as a separate disorder which usually occurs during periods of mental or physical stress. The eyes then feel tired and strained, focusing seems difficult and vision becomes less clear, especially during extensive detailed close work.

The more rare and serious defects include glaucoma (excessive pressure in the eyeball), cataract (opacity of the lens), conjunctivitis (inflammation of the outer layer), keratitis (inflammation of the cornea), and squint.[7]

The Bates Method is mainly concerned with errors of refraction, although it tends to have a beneficial effect on all functional and organic disorders of the eyes, including glaucoma, cataract and squint. Because the eyes are composed of living cells that constantly renew themselves, they respond to the needs of the organism and to changing conditions. What may look like an organic disorder and hopelessly beyond cure can often be affected by improved conditions (diet or way of life), proper functioning (exercises), or a new mental attitude towards the eyes and life in general. This last point is important because seeing is largely a mental process, and the eyes are really an extension of the brain. Their functioning and organic condition is greatly influenced by the mind. When blind people gain their eyesight through an operation, for example, they

34

cannot distinguish any objects at first, until the brain learns to interpret the images on the retina.

Short-sightedness (myopia) is more often found in children, and *far-sightedness* (hyperopia, hypermetropia and presbyopia) more often in older people. In the short-sighted eye the image falls short of the retina, and in the far-sighted eye it falls behind the retina. The fault lies either in the lens that does not accomodate enough, or in the shape of the eyeball that is either too long or too short.

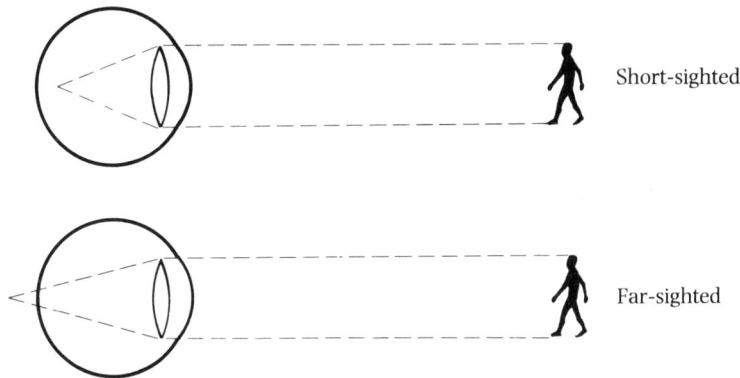

Short-sighted

Far-sighted

The short-sighted person can see near objects well but needs concave glasses to see distant objects. The far-sighted person can see far objects well but needs convex glasses to see near objects. But neither the far-sighted nor the near-sighted person can have perfect vision at any distance. Both of them see better at certain distances, but even then they do not see really well.

A person with *astigmatism* sees the world slightly distorted because the eyeball or the lens is not completely round. This can be corrected by prismatic lenses.

A person suffering from *glaucoma* is frequently not aware of this dangerous disease during the early stages. Pressure builds up inside the eyeball through blockage of outflow channels. There is no pain in the eye, but the internal pressure on the optic nerve can in time cause blindness. Glaucoma tends to occur in middle age or later, and it can be aggravated through emotions of excitement, fear, irritation, grief, strain or loss of a loved person – or through drugs like coffee.

Another serious disease is *cataract*, when the lens loses its transparency and becomes more and more opaque, often in old age or through diabetes. This is a biological change in the lens, not a growth. It is greatly affected by the person's general metabolic balance and responds to improved nutrition.

Conjunctivitis and *keratitis* are both inflammations, one of the outer skin of the visible eyeball, and the other of the cornea underneath. Both conditions are more likely to occur during periods of poor health, and the same applies to *sties*, an infection similar to acne of the many small glands around the eyelids.

The person with *squint* sees poorly because each eye looks in a different direction. Some babies are born with this condition. If it occurs later in life, the cause is usually lacking mental co-ordination.

Some people see tiny 'floating spots' in their field of vision. These are normally harmless and do not really interfere with clear vision. The text books are full of theories regarding their origin. According to some, they are caused by specks of debris floating in the jelly-like substance in front of the retina. Others state that the spots originate in the visual nerve centres of the brain.

The latter theory seems to be confirmed by the fact that the spots tend to disappear when the eyes are sharply focused on a particular object, and that they seem to multiply as soon as the eyes stare into space or on a white surface. Furthermore, the spots are mainly seen by intellectual people, and they can often by made to disappear through the methods of relaxation described in this book. Some people see the spots even when they close their eyes, which seems to indicate that they originate in the mind and not in the eyeball.

According to another theory the floating specks of debris .in front of the retina are impurities that can be reduced through proper nutrition and regular exercise.

About the up-dated Bates Method

Bates used the holistic approach to medicine. Instead of treating merely the one physical ailment of a patient, he looked at all aspects of the whole person. Before he specialized in ophthalmology he was trained as an M.D. For some years he worked as a research physician, and he discovered the extract that was later produced under the name of adrenalin. Through his experiments and research he came to the conclusion that faulty vision is most often a symptom of an underlying imbalance in the mind/body, and that it is almost invariably accompanied by mental strain.

He had a good intuitive understanding of how the human mind/body works. This, together with his thorough scientific investigations, made him one of the few real pioneers of medical science in modern times. After receiving his medical education at Cornell University he practiced ophthalmology for a number of years in New York City. Later he served for a time as clinical assistant at the Manhattan Eye and Ear Hospital, and as attending physician at Bellevue Hospital. At the age of 26 he became instructor in ophthalmology at the New York Postgraduate Medical School and Hospital. Five years later he gave up this post to do several years of experimental work, which enabled him to form the basis for his revolutionary theory.[8]

His followers have added to his theory. Aldous Huxley, for example, emphasized the mental and philosophical side of seeing, and Harry Benjamin stressed the importance of diet and balanced living.

I wrote the present book because I was impressed by the hidden potential in Dr Bates' theory, namely the effect of good vision on mental and physical well-being. In his book I came upon sentences like these:

"Doctor, thanks to you I am now seeing well again. But even more amazing is what you have done for my mind."

"As soon as the eyes are relaxed, the mind and body relax also."

"Then he saw the test chart clearly and distinctly again, and he immediately experienced a great feeling of relief. Every part of his body relaxed and all the previous mental tension seemed to dissolve."

In the course of his research Dr Bates found to his surprise that visual ability is closely linked to mental control. All aspects of mental and physical health are improved when the eyes function optimally. Even the other senses of touch, taste, hearing and smell become more discriminating when the eyes begin to see better. All parts of the body tend to function better, and the same is true of the digestive process. Any existing functional and organic illnesses tend to be relieved. Especially the ability to think clearly and efficiently is greatly increased.

Dr Bates' observations were so remarkable that I felt the subject deserved further investigation. An attempt in this direction is the present book which covers the more practical aspects of vision and the other benefits touched on by Bates: greater fitness, health and vitality, a feeling of mental and physical well-being, the ability to remember, imagine and think more clearly, and the ability to relax and to function more efficiently.

Critics of the Bates Method have said that it cannot possibly work because part of the underlying premise is incorrect. Most textbooks say that the eyes adjust to changing distance by changing the curvature of the lens. Because the lens tends to harden with age, and produce farsightedness, it is assumed that this cannot be corrected except through glasses.

But Bates had cured so many people of far-sightedness and presbyopia with his methods that he could not accept the prevailing theory. He concluded that the eye *can* accommodate by changing the shape of the eyeball, or that in most cases the eye can be trained to do so. He explained that the recti muscles that direct the eyes can also be taught to lengthen or flatten the eyeball slightly. By relaxing one pair of recti muscles and tensing another pair the shape of the eyeball can change a fraction of a millimetre, which is enough to let the image fall precisely on the retina.

If people can learn to wiggle their ears and widen their nostrils with practice, it seems likely that they can learn to influence the relative tension of their eye muscles. If they are properly instructed and motivated, the necessary nerve mechanism can establish itself in the brain. But as long as people believe that the proper way of dealing with poor eyesight is to buy a pair of glasses, their eyes will not learn to see without these artificial aids.

Dr Bates suffered from presbyopia himself. His eyes had lost all their accommodating power, and he had to carry around a whole assortment of glasses, one pair for each distance range. He realized that he could not expect others to accept his unorthodox theories if he could not cure himself. As long as he wore glasses, he was a living example for the failure of his theories.

He consulted several eye specialists. The verdict was invariably: "The lenses in your eyes are as hard as stone. Nobody can do anything for you." Then he went to a nerve specialist, who consulted his colleagues in turn. None of them could offer any useful ideas. After studying his own case extensively he discovered that his eyes accommodated after all, but always in the wrong way. He invented then various techniques to re-educate his eyes, and after six months he was able to read the newspapers without glasses. A year later he could even accommodate to distances between four and eighteen inches.

It seldom took Dr Bates that long to cure his patients, however. In some cases their eyes were completely and permanently cured within one hour. One patient who had worn glasses for presbyopia for about twenty years was improved in less than fifteen minutes. This man could hardly believe the sudden change, and thought at first that Dr Bates had hypnotized him. Such 'miracle cures' were rare, of course, and in nine cases out of ten the treatment extended over months.

In his book *The Art of Seeing*[9] Aldous Huxley relates how he was left near-blind at the age of sixteen, through opacities in the cornea and other complications. For eighteen months he had to depend on Braille for his reading, and he could not walk without a guide. Gradually he learned to read with a magnifying glass, and after some years he got used to wearing strong glasses. Eye strain and the accompanying mental exhaustion were a constant problem. At the age of 45 his vision began to fail again and decreased steadily.

At this point he happened to hear about the Bates Method of visual re-education, and about a teacher who used this method with remarkable success. Within months of beginning the training he was reading without glasses, and the previous strain and fatigue disappeared also. Even the opacity in the cornea cleared up to a great extent.

Aldous Huxley, the world famous author of more than thirty books and plays, was undoubtedly one of the great minds of the century. He had a habit of going to the crux of problems. With regard to the subject of vision he came to the conclusion that orthodox ophthalmologists did not accept the idea of vision training because they treated only the physiological aspect of seeing. They paid no attention to the mind of which the eyes are an instrument.

Huxley had been treated by some of the most prominent eye specialists of his time. None of them ever suggested to him that there might be a mental side to vision. None of them pointed out that there are right ways and wrong ways of using the eyes. They displayed great professional skill in examining his eyes and accurately diagnosed the symptoms of his disorder. Then they gave him some artificial lenses and let him go.

Ophthalmologists, on the other hand, can point to the fact that vision training is sometimes time consuming, and that results cannot be guaranteed. It requires the will to learn, strong motivation, patience and persistence, and faith in the body's regenerating powers. Some people simply seem to lack one or the other of these qualities, and no effort is made in school or elsewhere to develop them. Until simplified methods of vision training are devised and applied on a large scale, most people will be uninformed

40

enough to buy a pair of glasses at the slightest sign of decreasing sight – and opticians will be very happy to sell them the glasses.

Glasses, Contact Lenses, Sunglasses

At present, 52 per cent of the US population use corrective lenses, and this figure is expected to increase steadily in the coming years. Of the remaining 48 per cent most will use lenses later in life.

As any other marvel of technology, glasses can be a blessing, but they can also be a curse. They can be of great convenience to people whose vision is seriously impaired, but at the same time it must be admitted that they are bad for the eyes of most people. At best they are a necessary evil. They interfere with the self-regulating forces in the eye and the mind. Once the eyes get used to glasses, they no longer try to adjust, and the subnormal vision becomes permanent. Any unconscious attempt by the eyes to get back to normal is then frustrated, because when they focus correctly the world looks blurred through glasses.

People who have just bought their first pair of glasses can observe how their vision without glasses deteriorates within a few weeks. Where before they could not see very well without glasses, they now find that their vision has become even more subnormal. People who lose or break their glasses, on the other hand, can observe how their eyesight without glasses improves within a week or two.

Glasses are like crutches: they make a weak organ more usable, but they weaken it further. Some people are forced to wear crutches or glasses because their organs are inherently weak or crippled. But the average pair of eyes does not fall into this category. Almost invariably, the cause of poor vision is found in an imbalance of the mind/ body. If glasses would really improve the eyes, a person wearing them would see better after a while and finally see best without them. But the opposite usually happens: glasses have to be replaced by stronger ones periodically.

Many text books on ophthamology state that corrective

lenses can neither weaken or strengthen the eyes. At the same time they admit that it is best to use the weakest possible prescription at any given time, to retard the process of deteriorating eyesight. They say, in other words, that strong glasses speed up the process of deterioration. They also admit that the ability to accomodate is often influenced by moods and nervous conditions. Through such contradictory statements they simultaneously confirm and reject the Bates Method, and they are unable to explain why this method has helped hundreds of thousands to improve their eyesight.

Many disadvantages of wearing glasses and contact lenses can be listed. They limit the field of vision to the area seen through the lenses. They change the size of the object seen, enlarging it in the case of far-sightedness and reducing it in the case of short-sightedness. They reduce or distort colour vision. They tend to lose part of their transparency through dust, condensation and other pollutants, and have to be cleaned frequently. They make a person accident-prone and more likely to overlook advancing road traffic.

Finally, glasses always disfigure a face more or less, it spite of the advertisements by optical manufacturers who try to convince us that people wearing glasses look more glamorous and intelligent. Most children know better than that – they don't want to be seen wearing glasses, and they feel that there is something wrong with people who wear them. If despite improvement in your eyesight from the Bates Method you should feel 'naked' without glasses, perhaps the solution would be to buy a pair with plain glass.

Another undesirable effect of glasses was discovered after Dr Bates did his research. It relates to the need of the eyes for full-spectrum daylight, as will be explained in the next chapter. Most glasses, sunglasses and contact lenses filter out much of the spectrum and deprive the mind/body of certain essential light waves. Sunglasses further cause the pupils to stay open in bright light, which allows certain undesirable light waves to enter. Full-spectrum sunglasses are now available, but visors, sunshades or hats are normally preferable. Sunglasses become necessary only in conditions of strong glare from below, or when sunlight is reflected from snow or water. People with normal vision are not normally irritated by daylight anyway, and they have no need for protection, unless they feel ill or temporarily nervous.

Many people are in favour of contact lenses because they seem less cumbersome and disfiguring, Although they cost many times as much and need careful maintenance, they make a person feel more secure and attractive. The new 'soft lenses' cost even more and wear out after a year or two. Unfortunately, all contact lenses add another nuance to the strain in the eye which causes or accompanies poor vision in the first place. Furthermore, they normally stay in place all day, while glasses can easily be taken off now and then to relax and exercise the eyes. (All exercises recommended in later chapters should be done without lenses).

Manufacturers and sellers of optical lenses will not agree with the Bates Method. They operate a profitable business, and they do not like to be told that their products are useless or even harmful. They can point to the fact that the general public likes to buy glasses and has no time for vision training. Most people have never heard of the method, and they wouldn't want to bother with it even if they did hear about it. There is some truth in this line of reasoning, especially since lenses are promoted by million dollar advertising campaigns, while the Bates Method is not promoted because 'there is no money in it'. (Only one country promotes vision training on a large scale today: China).

Eye specialists, on the other hand, who are better informed and have no vested interests in the optical industry, tend to down-grade the Bates Method for another reason. Patients come to them looking for quick relief of their symptoms, and they almost expect to get glasses prescribed because they do not know better. The eye specialists have been trained to investigate the eyes only, and they have no time or inclination to look into the intricate relation between eyes, mind and body. Even if they did have the time, the patient may not want to pay for a thorough diagnosis and lengthy treatment. In the end, the average patient gets the treatment that Aldous Huxley described: ". . . they gave me some artificial lenses and let me go."

Many opticians and ophthalmologists will reject the Bates Method simply because they wear glasses – which marks them as sufferers from mental strain, according to Bates. They could not very well recommend the method when their own eyes still need glasses.

How Light Affects Your Eyes

The eyes function best under normal lighting conditions on a normal day, and sunlight is their element. If they are deprived of light for several months, they turn temporarily blind. The same happens if they look straight into the sun. Horses working in mines can no longer see, and people who watch the eclipse of the sun with the bare eye can lose their sight.

Normal eyes thrive on a healthy balance between light and shade, night and day. They need sunlight to stimulate the nerves of the retina, and to increase the blood circulation in and around the eyes. They also need to rest during the darkness of night. Through millions of years of evolution, the human eye has adapted to this cycle, and there is no reason to believe that it is in any way harmful or that the eyes must be protected from sunlight.

But people with imperfect vision find sunlight irritating, and this is one of the reasons why sunglasses are getting more popular every year. To protect the eyes from 'harmful' sunlight is considered 'the smart thing to do', and optical manufacturers encourage this illusion by picturing people in glamorous settings wearing these glasses.

Sensitivity to light is the first sign of strain or illness and this is often connected with a person's posture, with the postion of neck and head. When the head is stretched forward, the lower eyelids have to be raised in order to shut out part of the light, and this causes 'screwing' and tension around the eyes. The Japanese have a word for it, 'sanpaku', which can be translated as 'accident-prone'. When a person's head is lowered and stretched forward so that the white of the eyeball shows underneath the iris, he/she is said to be sanpaku and liable to get into all kinds of trouble, even including violent death. This confirms what Bates said about the bad effects of strain in all areas of life. As mentioned in Chapter 12, spinal rigidity and bad posture are part of this picture.

On abnormally bright days, or when light is reflected from snow or water, some protection may be desirable, but eyeshades, visors or hats are better than sunglasses as explained in the last chapter. During illness or after excessive consumption of alcohol, nicotine and certain other drugs, the eyes may also be abnormally sensitive to light, and needing protection.

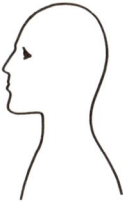

Head balancing on top of spine, white not showing below the iris, and upper lids can shut out light if necessary.

Strained position of head and eyes, with white showing underneath the iris, or raised lower lids.

To see well and without discomfort in bright condition, the eyes have to be healthy and relaxed. Dr Bates found that the same is also true for subnormal or adverse lighting conditions. He made the astonishing discovery that people with good vision can read small print in dim light, in moving vehicles or in a lying position, without discomfort and without harm to the eyes. He even found that reading under these unfavourable conditions benefits the eyes, *as long as they stay relaxed*. This is because the eyes can read small print in dim light only if they function without effort, and with central fixation, while well illuminated large print can also be read by tense eyes. Adverse conditions are a challenge to healthy eyes, while ideal conditions may tempt them to function inefficiently. The same applies to reading in bed or in a moving vehicle, when conditions are not ideal and the eyes can see well only when they function effortlessly. This is also good mental training, since it trains the mind to adjust to all kinds of circumstances.

This should not be carried to the extremes, however. Chances are that your vision is not perfect, and that poor illumination *and other adverse conditions* might add to the already existing strain in your eyes. Normally it is a good idea to have a strong light shine on the object you are looking at, to illuminate also the background, and to avoid having light shine into your eyes. Television sets, for example, should not be watched in total darkness, but with a dimly lit background. Lamps should be placed behind or above you, so that they do not shine directly into your eyes. When reading out-of-doors, do not place the page into direct sunlight but in the shade. Natural light is better than artificial light, and conditions for reading are best when you sit near a large window but facing away from it, so that bright indirect light falls on the page but not into your eyes.

With regard to the quality of light, researchers have recently found that the body needs the full spectrum of natural sunlight, unfiltered by glass, to function properly. Sunlight is not only needed by the skin to form Vitamin D, which in turn keeps the bones strong and resilient, but it also stimulates certain photoreceptors in the eyes. Only a small part of the sun's spectrum is visible, but the invisible rays enter the eyes nevertheless. They stimulate the retina which sends nervous impulses to various parts of the brain, to the hypothalamus, and to the pituitary and pineal glands which control the body metabolism. Dozens of research institutions are accumulating evidence to this effect, among them the Centre for Light Research in Fort Lauderdale and the Laboratory for Environmental Physics in Triangle Park, North Carolina. Dr John Ott, who established the first mentioned institute, was one of the pioneers in this field. He produced several fascinating slow-motion films showing the effect of sunlight (or lack of it) on growing plants. Invariably, the plants raised under artificial light (especially neon light) or behind glass windows showed various defects. Some plants would fail to produce seeds or flowers, others would produce only weak shoots that wilted away, and some would not grow at all. Some of his experimental plants had been placed close to a colour television set by co-incidence, and they also suffered. Rats and guinea pigs exposed to the same conditions lost hair, became impotent, turned neurotic or apathetic, etc.[10]

Plain sunlight, which we have taken for granted until now, is gradually being recognised as an essential nutrient. Just as some people suffer from malnutrition and others from Vitamin deficiency, some of us will be diagnosed as suffering from 'spectrum deficiency'. Fifty years ago, lack of sunlight was discovered to be the cause of rickets, which had deformed millions of children up to that time. Now we may have to add to this list all kinds of mental and physical imbalances. Full-spectrum lamps will become more common in homes and at places of work. Plexiglass and other plastic windows that let the sunlight through will replace many a glass window. People will be more weary of spectacles and contact lenses that deprive their eyes of the full sunlight, or they will buy special full-spectrum glasses.* They will also try to spend more time outdoors.

---

*Full-spectrum lenses can be ordered through optometrists from Armolite Lens Co., P.O.Box 1038, Burbank, CA 91505.
Full-spectrum contact lenses are available from Milton Roy Co., P.O. Box 1899, Sarasota, Fla. 33578.
Full-spectrum lamps are made by Duro-Lite Corporation, 1710 Willow Street, Fair Lawn, N.J. 07410.

The Eyesight of Children

According to many textbooks, the eyes evolved mainly for the purpose of distant vision, and too much close work harms them. Our ancestors needed their eyes for hunting or spotting of predators and enemies, not for reading or making small objects. Poor vision is thus the price we have to pay for the benefits of civilization, and glasses are the badges of civilization.

This theory persists in spite of the fact that it was shown to be incorrect many years ago. Most primitive people do a great deal of close work when preparing food, eating, weaving, making pottery and producing other implements. But the important thing is how they do it. In their youth they are not forced, like our modern children, to spend half the day indoors sitting in rigid positions. They are not made to memorize, under threat of punishment, things that scem irrelevant and boring to them. They are not forced to compete with each other and to succeed at tasks that mean little or nothing to them. They are not herded into large classes and supervised by authoritarian instructors. Their instructors are not part of a learning situation which makes them and their pupils nervous and irritable, and which fosters dishonesty, obstinacy and deviousness in the pupils. At home after school they are not tempted to spend hours sitting in front of the television set which presents them with scenes of sensless violence.

When children from illiterate societies are exposed to these conditions, they usually develop poor vision within weeks, and have to wear glasses. This is not because they have to read too much but because they live under constant mental strain. Teachers have often observed that their pupils can see the blackboard quite well at the beginning of each term, but that their vision deteriorates as the weeks go by. Dr Bates tells of one case where a teacher explained the process of vision to her pupils and showed them how they could rest and improve their eyes with the help of a Snellen test card placed on the wall. None of her pupils developed defective vision.

But when the method was introduced on a large scale in some schools of New York City, many teachers applied it improperly or not at all, and the experiment was abandoned. The method was then tried in other cities with more success, after the teachers had been more thoroughly informed. In all cases, the vision of the average pupil improved substantially. If this program had been further perfected and made part of the curriculum, fewer children would have to wear glasses today. But after a time the orthodox forces in the school system prevailed. Instead of setting aside a few minutes a day to show children how to use their eyes, modern teachers cram a few more irrelevant facts into the heads of their pupils.

This is where parents can often help. They can find out if their children have visual difficulties at school or elsewhere, and they can take appropriate measures. Quite often the children are not aware of their own troubles. They may not know the difference between normal and subnormal vision, and they may assume that the letters on the blackboard 'are' blurred.

But can people survive in modern society without the knowledge they acquire in school? Children should acquire knowledge, of course, and they are born with a natural urge to learn. Just like kittens, they are naturally curious, they want to know about important things. They continually pester their parents with 'silly questions'. They want to know where we come from, why the sky is blue, why grown-ups wear glasses, why some things float in the bath tub while others sink, why girls look different from boys, why rainbows are colourful, and why they have to go to bed at night. This is what biology, physics, chemistry, history, etc. is really all about. Nothing could make children more happy than to have these things explained to them, at their own level and in their own terms.

Children also learn by following the example of those grown-ups whom they love. They automatically reject the teachings of people whom they dislike. What they learn in school under duress does not really become integrated into their store of practical knowledge, and after a few years of coercive 'learning' they have lost their natural urge to acquire essential knowledge and to use their minds creatively.

That teaching can be done without the coercive method has been proven by the many schools established by A. S. Neill, Rudolf Steiner and others.[11] As soon as teachers learn to present the material in interesting ways, most pupils consider going to class as a privilege and a pleasure. Those children who are more practically inclined and less interested in abstract knowledge should be encouraged to develop their talents in practical fields. Playing should form a large part of the curriculum. Girls learn to be mothers by playing with dolls, just as kittens learn to catch mice by playing with balls of cotton. The urge to play is part of the urge to learn, and by discouraging one we would discourage the other.

Einstein's teacher told him that he would never amount to much because he showed little interest in the curriculum. But Einstein had an uncontrollable desire to find out how Nature works. Every child has such an interest of one kind or another, which tends to get buried by our clumsy educational system. Children should also be shown the virtues of patience, hard work and discipline, which they will need at times. None of these virtues imply mental strain, however. Just as our eyes see best when they function easily and spontaneously, so our mind and body are most efficient and successful when they function joyously and are motivated by a worthwhile goal. To endure stress is sometimes necessary, but to strain habitually day after day drains our vitality, decreases our vision and brings on psycho-somatic troubles.

Part Two

Ways of Improving Vision and Well-Being

Resting the Eyes (Palming, Sunning)

Like all other organs, the eyes need periodic rest. They also function best in a state of 'restful alertness' or 'dynamic relaxation' because of their subtle and complex construction. Any mental strain is felt as a strain on the eyes, and anything that relaxes the eyes also calms the mind.

In all cultures and ages, people have known the value of periodic withdrawal when they felt the need to find themselves and to regain their mental focus. This kind of voluntary 'sensory deprivation' can have a healing effect by shutting out distracting influences for a while. People find it easiest to meditate in quiet places where they will not be disturbed, under subdued lighting conditions, and with closed eyes.

In our hectic modern age we tend to lose touch with ourselves. Our five senses are glued to the ever-changing man-made scenes and artificial diversions around us. Our sense of sight tends to get over-loaded with irrelevant stimuli. All this can contribute to faulty thinking, bodily ills and faulty vision.

One of the simplest and most effective methods for resting the eyes and the mind is called 'palming'. The palms of the hands are used to cover the closed eyes (remove glasses or lenses first!). Each palm covers one eyeball without touching it, and the fingers of both hands cross on the forehead. Thus all light is effectively shut out, which cannot be done by a mere closing of the eyelids. The warmth of the palms radiates on the eyes and gives a feeling of peace and protection. People often assume this posture instinctively when they feel tired or ill. Proponents of natural healing methods believe that the hands possess special curative powers.

You would normally palm for several minutes and up to one hour, by sitting up in bed or by resting the elbows on a

55

table or firm pillow. If you see images of floating clouds, flashing lights or coloured patches, don't worry about them. They are symptoms of an underlying strain, and any effort to make them go away would only cause further strain.

Simply relax completely and imagine pleasant scenes in motion, like flying birds, cornfields waving in the breeze, running animals or sailing boats moving through gentle waves. Now and then you can also picture black objects moving about, such as a black cat, a black crow or a black vehicle. To avoid 'mental staring' it is best to imagine scenes in motion, with the following exception.

When you open your eyes for a few seconds during palming sessions, look at an EYE-Q Chart placed in front of you and notice how black the letters are on it. Printer's ink is about the blackest thing on earth. Focus on the large Y in the upper left corner and see how black it is. Look at every part of it and convince yourself that every part is black. Now close your eyes and see the letter in your mind, totally black, for a fraction of a second. Open they eyes for a moment and ponder the black once more. Then continue palming for a few minutes, always in a relaxed frame of mind, and imagining pleasant scenes in motion.

Now and then you may fall from this state of dynamic relaxion into a state of passive relaxation, when your eyes turn up spontaneously and become almost immobile. You are then looking at your eyebrows from the inside, so to speak, and you are on the verge of sleep. This state is actually more restful than certain phases of sleep. The dream state, for example, is accompanied by rapid eye movements ('REM'), when your eyes are following the drama of your dream as it unfolds.

Dr Bates tells of a man nearly seventy years old who was suffering from astigmatism, presbyopia and incipient cataract. For twenty years he had worn different glasses for near and far vision, but now the cataract was clouding his view. Other eye specialists had offered no hope, except through an operation of the cataract. Dr Bates gave him instructions in palming and asked him to come back a few days later. The patient was so enthusiastic that he spent the whole next day palming, from early morning to midnight, only stopping to drink water in between. He found this quite exhausting. But when he looked at the test card he found that he could see normally again, and that he could read fine print. Even the clouds in the lenses had receded. There was no relapse in the following years.

Normal vision has been restored in many other cases after a few sessions of palming. But if you should find that you belong to a small percentage of people who are not benefited by palming, you should try the other methods described in this book first.

Whether you use the palming technique for short or long periods depends on your schedule and the urgency of your case. You may want to space short sessions through the day, or have only one longer session if you don't find this too tedious. You may also find that you enjoy the sessions when you imagine certain scenes, and not so much when you picture others. By experimenting you can develop a convenient daily routine. A steady continuous daily programme brings the best results, which may even include the disappearance of other seemingly unrelated discomforts in your body. The more you gain a sense of well-being during each session, the longer this feeling will last afterwards.

Whenever you find it inconvenient or embarrassing to do the actual palming, you can gain some benefits also by simply closing your eyes and doing the usual picturing of scenes. When circumstances make even such 'mental palming' impossible, it helps to close the eyes now and then for a few seconds, and to blink more often. You can go through the day much more relaxed if you keep this in mind, and if you also keep your eyelids partly closed most of the time. You see the world just as clearly through drooping eyelids, and you will be less likely to stare.

But all this is no substitute for the actual palming. The sessions may appear time consuming at first, but they are in fact a good investment. You may feel that time is money, that you have more important things to do, that you must get ahead, be successful, keep up with the Joneses, take care of the family, etc. If you become a nervous wreck in the process and spend a fortune on doctors and hospitals, that cannot be helped, you may say. If you lose your peace of mind and send out destructive vibrations at home and at work, that's bad luck. If your life is out of focus and you keep stumbling into accidents, that's the way things happen. But one day you realize that one ounce of prevention is better than a pound of cure – and that an hour's relaxation is better than a week in hospital.

When you close your eyes and cover them with your palms for a minute, what do you see? Coloured spots, moving patterns, bursting stars? Or do you see nothing but black? Only people with perfect vision see black. Shapes and colours are produced by disturbances in the visual centres of the brain, they are illusions. Any disturbances of mind or body, such as fatigue, hunger, anger, worry or depression tends to multiply such illusions. The better your vision, the more perfect is the black you see. If you normally have perfect vision and you notice coloured patterns while palming, you know that these are the first signs of illness or other imbalance. What easier way is there to monitor your health now and then? This warning signal gives you time to look at your present living habits and the condition of your mind/body, and to prevent a possibly serious development. How much black did you see in today's session? Enter your findings in the Palming Progress Chart in the back of the book, and do this periodically in the future.

Some people feel that their eyes emit light rays, much as a flash-light emits a beam of light. Even Plato was convinced of this. They feel that they must actively direct this beam in the desired direction, and that they can turn it off by closing their eyelids. In this they are confirmed by figures of speech like: 'beaming eyes', 'the sparkle is someone's eyes', or 'hate shooting from his eyes'. But all such sparks, beams and rays are only in the mind of the beholder. The eyes are passive organs in most respects, and the retina in the back of the eye is no more active that a photo-electric cell. Even the focusing is done unconsiously and does not need conscious effort. The more the eyes are left to themselves, the better they function. By remembering this you will find it easier to relax your mind, your body and your eyes. Through exercises like palming you can further regain the ability to see without effort. Your palming will be even more successful after you have proven to yourself that you see best without strain, and that strain is bad for your eyes.

Sunning

You can enhance the benefits of palming by exposing your closed eyes to the sun or a sun lamp for several minutes before each session. Direct light of the rising or setting sun, unfiltered by window glass is best. Find a comfortable seat, take your glasses off, close your eyes and face the sun. Gently move your head sideways and up and down, so that the rays meet your face from all angles. If the sun should at first irritate your eyes and make them water, cover one eye at a time with one hand and then the other. All people with impaired vision have a nervous fear of the sun, which disappears as they learn to relax.

If you live in a zone where the sun shines less often, or you have not time during the day, you can use an ordinary sun lamp placed at a comfortable distance. A 'full spectrum' lamp would be better, as explained in How Light Affects Your Eyes, page 46.

After the sunning, gently massage your face around the eyes, but resist the temptation to rub itchy eyelids. Picture the eyeballs in your mind, and 'talk' to them. Tell them that they are doing a splendid job, that you need them and love them, and that you will do your best to supply them with clean nutrients and oxygen. Visualize the interior of the eyes, the lens and the retina, and the muscles surrounding the eyeballs. Sense the millions of living cells that are busily maintaining all parts of the eyes in good condition, and the blood stream that constantly feeds the cells. Remember how the sun's rays warm and stimulate the eyes, and how the palming relaxes them.

Keeping the Eyes Mobile (Shifting, Blinking)

Most people assume that their eyes see more or less equally well at all times, and that they see best when they look firmly at each object.

Nothing could be further from the truth. The focus and the direction of healthy eyes shift continuously. Within a single second, they may shift a dozen times. This corresponds to the restless activity of the brain, of which the eyes are an extension. The human brain is forever comparing, evaluating, judging, imagining and remembering at an incredible rate, performing hundreds of complex operations each minute.

When you look at the headline on this page, for example, your eyes scan over the letters with lightning speed, touching several points within each letter, all in about one second. When you look up from the book and let your eyes roam over the furniture or other objects in front of you, your eyes flit over the scene and adjust for distance with each shift. All these simultaneous adjustments and scanning motions are steered from the brain, and they are astonishingly accurate when mind and eyes are well balanced. But even in the best eyes they cannot be perfect at all times. Each little movement or shift throws the eyes somewhat out of focus. Nobody has perfect vision for more than a minute or two. Mobility and instability are inherent in the eyes as well as the mind, and adjustment is largely achieved by a continuous and automatic process of trial and error.

This is one of the first things people with defective vision have to understand before they can expect any improvement. Almost invariably, their vision is accompanied and made worse by their habit of staring and of expecting to see equally well at all times. They have to acquire mental and visual mobility.

If the eyes cannot maintain perfect vision for more than a few minutes, it is equally true that poor vision is not poor all the time. All persons with errors of refraction have, now and then, moments of normal vision. Even the form of the error changes, so that a far-sighted person may become near-sighted for a second, or vice-versa. Throughout the day, a person's eyesight changes continuously. Vision may be good in the morning and poor in the evening, or it may be good while aimed at one object and poor when perceiving another. School children may be so myopic in the class room that they cannot see the blackboard, but when they go fishing in the afternoon they may see quite well at any distance. People who are asked to read the Snellen Test Card by an optician may feel so apprehensive that they become near-sighted or far-sighted for the moment, and are then diagnosed as having poor vision and needing glasses.

Aside from the fact that some people buy glasses needlessly, there is another aspect to consider when wearing glasses. As the eyes get used to the additional lenses, they try less often to see well without them. But if they do make the attempt and succeed in accomodating perfectly, the world will seem blurred through the glasses, and they will soon give up further attempts. The self-regulating and recuperative powers of the eyes are effectively neutralized by glasses and contact lenses. This is why people who want to improve their vision should take them off whenever possible, or wear a slightly weaker prescription.

When you look at an unfamiliar or unpleasant object, your eyesight usually becomes less keen. You may have found that you left museums and supermarkets with slightly blurred vision, because your eyes could not take in the overwhelming variety of unfamiliar sights. The same can happen when you travel in strange surroundings or come upon unpleasant sights. Even loud or unusual noises can throw your eyes out of focus. When you visit the city after having lived in a quiet country environment, you will tend to see less clearly. Your eyes may react the same way when you feel threatened or endangered in any way, or when you worry about real or imaginary problems. Any imbalance in the mind/body can cause or increase poor vision: mental or physical discomfort, pain, fever, anxiety, anger, etc. Some of these factors will be discussed in later chapters.

All these states are invariably accompanied by strain and immobility in the eyes. While healthy eyes shift and adjust effortlessly and continuously, defective eyes move awkwardly, with effort and less often. You can do three exercises to promote the mobility and effortless co-ordination in your eyes: blinking, shifting and flashing.

Blinking

People with imperfect vision move their eyes less often and they also blink less often. Eyeballs and eyelids seem to be steered from the same nerve centre in the brain, which can tense up and function less efficiently at times. By consciously making the eyelids blink more often you achieve a relaxing effect on the eyes. At the same time you help the eyelids perform their natural function, of course, which is to clean and lubricate the eyes, and to keep them moist for better transparency. With each closing of the eyelids, the eyes are also rested for a moment, which is beneficial.

How often do you blink in one minute? Five times, ten times, twenty times or more often? Once every three seconds or twenty times per minute would be about normal. Time yourself and enter the result in the Blinking Progress Chart in back of the book. Monitor your blinking frequency periodically in the coming weeks.

Chances are that you sometimes stare at the world around you, and forget to blink, while at the same time you may also forget to breathe. Especially while reading, driving and watching television, your eyes may temporarily freeze. Be also aware of your eyes when you talk to other people. You'll be surprised to discover how often human beings stare at each other.

Take a full minute now and then to do some quick and easy blinking. Close the eyes for a few seconds and then let them blink again like a butterfly. Repeat this several times a day, and develop your eye-awareness.

Flashing

By glancing quickly at an object and then closing the eyes again, you can usually get a sharper image of the object than by watching it in the normal way. Instead of actively straining, you take relaxed flashes, so to speak. You can practice flashing while you are engaged in your everyday activities at home and at work. Develop the habit of taking rapid glances at things, of closing the eyes momentarily and remembering what you have seen. This will give you a relaxed sense of detachment. You can also set aside a few minutes every day to practice flashing with the EYE-Q Chart or small and familiar objects, like dice or dominoes.

When using dice, throw three or four of them, glance quickly at them, and close your eyes and picture the numbers in your mind. This exercise may work best if someone else throws the dice and covers them after a second.

When using dominoes, arrange nine of them in three rows of three at a distance where you can conveniently see them. After closing your eyes, glance at one row of three dominoes at a time. (You have six choices, three horizontal and three vertical rows.) Close the eyes again after a second and picture the white dots you saw.

Shifting

As mentioned above, your eyes see best when they are constantly shifting. As soon as they focus on one point for longer that a fraction of a second, they begin to strain and to see less. If you look, for example, at the full stop at the end of the last sentence for one whole minute, your eyes will either shift in a continuous motion inside and around the dot – or they will become immobile and produce a blurred image within a few seconds.

To develop the habit of keeping the eyes mobile in a relaxed way, you can practice several shifting exercises. These are done with the test card, by shifting the eyes from one letter to another. At this point it is necessary to men-tion the phenomenon of 'central fixation', which will be fully explained in a later chapter. In short, it means that people with imperfect vision do not see the point at which they are looking as sharply as other points near it. At night, for example, they may see a certain star best when they look at another star nearby. When they look at the test card, they may look at one letter but see the one next to it more sharply. They should therefore do their shifting exercises by shifting between letters that are a little farther removed from each other, so that the 'central fixation' factor is eliminated.

By shifting your eyes in this way, back and forth between two letters, both letters will appear blacker and sharper. In other words, your vision will improve. The more normal your vision becomes, the more you will notice one other phenomenon: As you shift your eyes to one side, the letters seem to be moving in the opposite side. As you shift your eyes back and forth between the letters, the test card will seem to swing back and forth in the opposite direction. But you will not notice this as long as your vision is below normal.

People with poor vision perceive the test card as being stationary or as moving in the same direction as the shifting eyes.

The following exercises are often more successful after resting the eyes by closing them or palming, although the shifting itself is also restful to the eyes. By alternately palming and shifting, a temporary or permanent improvement is often achieved in a few weeks. If this method produces no prompt results, the other exercises described in this book should be tried first.

a. Look at a letter on the EYE-Q Chart. Shift to another letter on the same line, then back and forth, until both of them improve and begin to swing in the direction opposite to your eye movements.

b. Look at a large letter, then shift to a small one further down the chart. Then repeat as above, for half a minute.

c. Look at a large letter, and shift between its upper and lower end. Repeat as above.

d. Shift between two charts, one placed near and the other farther away, alternating between the same letter.

e. Picture two letters on the test card in your mind, and shift mentally between them. Try to use smaller and smaller letters. Some people find this easier than visual shifting.

f. When reading, let your eyes scan over and around each word, switching back and forth through the letters.

Shifting can also be done without a test card, of course. You can shift between two books on the shelf, two dice, two windows in a distant building, two stars, or even between two letters on this page.

When watching television, let your eyes roam over the screen and off the screen. Let them wander around the edges of objects instead of fixing them near the centre. Practice 'edging' also in your daily life whenever you can, at home, at work, in the bus, at the cinema and in other places.

If you are far-sighted or short-sighted, shift between near and far objects whenever you have an opportunity, (as in exercise d.). One of the best ways to improve your power of accomodation is to move an object toward the eyes and away from them, in an even rhythm for several minutes. You can, for instance, move one hand back and forth between the tip of your nose and the stretched-arm position, or you can move a stick between your nose and away from it. Tossing a small ball or an apple into the air and following it with your eyes up and down for a few minutes has a similar effect. Playing frisbee also helps the eyes. Whenever you can, follow such exercises with a few minutes of palming.

The more awareness of the fact that shifting improves vision while staring reduces it has helped many people to see better.

Keeping Flexible (Swinging)

The last chapter explained how your eyes function best when they are mobile and relaxed. But your eyes can be mobile only when your body is flexible and alive. Staring and poor vision are almost always associated with a certain rigidity of the neck and the spine. While the eyes are one extension of the brain, the nerves inside the spine are another, and both interrelate to some extent. People like chiropractors who make a thorough study of the spine know that the poor vision of a patient is sometimes cured after spinal manipulation. Practitioners of the Alexander Technique of postural integration* have found that especially shortsighted people tend to have bad posture, and that vision and posture can often be improved simultaneously. People who go through life with an over-anxious attitude tend to stare and stretch the head forward, which bends the spine and tenses the neck. One chiropractor said that he could determine the degree of a person's emotional problems by looking at a lateral X-Ray of his/her neck.

Oriental teachings have emphasized for thousands of years that flexibility means life while rigidity means death. Lao Tzu observes in the Tao Te Ching that we enter the world supple and leave it rigid. The Oriental martial arts teach the virtues of agility and flexibility, of moving like a willow rather than an oak. They show that brute force most often leads to defeat, while a flexible and yielding use of power leads to victory.

The Yogis of ancient India considered spinal flexibility an indispensable pre-requisite for mental and physical health, and many of the Yoga exercises are devised especially for this purpose. Even our modern astronauts practice Yoga

---

*The Alexander Technique by Sarah Barker (Bantam Books) seems to be the best book on the subject.

exercises when they have to spend several days in a space capsule. Their doctors found that the body cannot retain its flexibility longer than 48 hours without exercise, and that it needs a minimum of twenty minutes exercise per day.

Modern man lives in many ways like an astronaut, sitting indoors at home, in the car and at work, and staring at instruments or papers much of the time. Those of us who do not engage in daily compensating activities to keep flexible must bear the consequences. Medical research has proven beyond doubt that most of our modern diseases are brought on, directly or indirectly, by under-exercising and over-eating. Modern man is literally a 'sitting duck' for premature ageing, coronary heart disease, stroke, varicose veins, arthritis, diabetes, hypertension, liver disease, blood vessel degeneration, nervous troubles – and subnormal vision.

Even people whose work is physical do not always get balanced exercise. Their routine often requires special movements that stress one part of the body while it leaves another part slack. One of the most popular exercises to-day is jogging, which is sometimes advertised as a cure-all. Jogging can be beneficial if practiced in the right spirit and in moderation, but heart specialist Dr Christian Barnard called it 'a dangerous mania that can promote heart attack'. A more relaxed and balanced version of jogging is called skipping. This method is as old as mankind, and you can often see children skipping on the streets, in yards, and indoors. For them it is an expression of joy: skipping along in a kind of double step dance, solo or with others, straight or in circles, or even on the spot, right left, left right, right left, left right . . . . It is as much fun to do as to watch, for all children between the ages of five and ninety. It makes you feel good while other exercises tend to make you feel frustrated. You skip in graceful horizontal curves that gently exercise your whole body, while the jogger engages in jerky up-and-down movements.

The Elephant Swing

This pleasant exercise keeps your whole body flexible and

relaxes you at the same time. You should do it preferably outdoors or in front of an open window. Stand with your feet about eighteen inches apart and swing gently from side to side. You may have seen elephants in the zoo do this sort of swinging. Let your arms hang down loosely. Relax your mind, body and eyes completely and swing slowly, each side taking about one second (count 'seventy-one' to the left and again 'seventy-one' to the right, to get the right speed at first). Your whole rump, neck and head twists with each swing, so that you actually look behind you each time. When you swing to the left, let your right heel rise slightly, and vice versa. Your eyes are completely at rest, they do not look at anything in particular but just 'let the world pass by' with each swing. After a few minutes you will get 'into the swing' and continue automatically. You will feel a calming effect on your whole nervous system and the eyes after a while. Swing for five or ten minutes, two or three times a day, or whenever your eyes feel tense. For all exercises take off your glasses, of course.

As in the shifting exercises described in the last chapter, people with normal vision find that the scene in front of them seems to rush from side to side in the opposite direc-

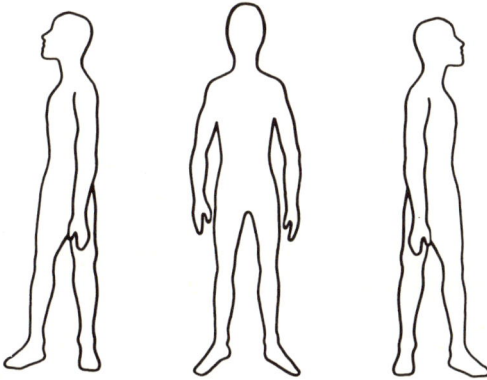

tion of each swing. You will get the same sensation as your vision improves. Don't forget to blink often while you swing. Close your eyes now and then and picture in your mind how the scene moves back and forth with each swing. The gentle rocking motion has a profound calming effect and it also stimulates the breathing. At the same time it gently exercises each vertebrae and increases the blood circulation around the spine.

The Short Swing

A good way to loosen the neck muscles while you train your eyes is the 'short swing', which you can practice sitting down. Find a place from which you can see far and near objects at the same time, for example a vase in the foreground and a garden in the background, or the vertical bar in a window and a landscape in back of it. Sit in an upright but relaxed position and turn the head slowly from side to side, without looking at any object in particular, just as with the elephant swing described above. As the scene rushes back and forth in front of you, the near objects seem to move faster than the distant ones. You can vary this routine by bending head and neck sideways instead of turning around. Do the short swing for a minute with open eyes, then with closed eyes and picturing the swinging scene in your mind, also for a minute.

Another way to keep the neck flexible is to rotate the head in a wide circular motion, several times around, first in one direction and then in the other. You can easily do this in the course of the day, while sitting at the desk, reading or watching television, or at any other time. Straighten your neck and spine afterwards, and let your head balance on top instead of stretching it forward. By carrying the head in this relaxed position, you automatically relax your eyes. You may also feel a pleasant tingling in the neck which results from relaxing the muscles and stimulating the blood circulation.

Eye Exercises

The muscles around the eyeballs should also be kept flexible and relaxed. They have to be in top shape to perform the intricate task of directing both eyes in unison. With many people today, these muscles atrophy to some extent,

70

they get lazy and weak. With other people they get hard and tense, and lose their ability to adjust. According to Bates, these muscles are also partly responsible for distance accomodation. Whenever you have a chance during the day or in the evening before falling asleep, give them a good workout by moving the eyeballs up and down and sideways as far as you can. Look down at your lips and tongue, up at your eybrows, and sideways at your temples. Roll them in a circular motion to the right and then to the left. Close the eyes and move them in a wide figure eight, first a lying eight and then a standing eight. Now describe a large square with your eyes, then a triangle. Exercise the eyelids also, by squeezing them shut tightly and then opening them wide (but never rub the eyes). Keep the eyes relaxed at all times and do some palming in between exercises.

Keep your spine flexible and test your spinal flexibility now and then through the following exercises, and enter results in the progress chart in back of the book.

a. Lie on your back, fold hands around knees, rock forward and backward, touching the ground with your feet in front and next to your head alternately, about ten times.

b. Sit on a bed, put this book opened directly behind you. Turn your head and try to see as much of the book as possible. Look first over one shoulder, then the other, then under each shoulder, several times.

Visualizing (The Black Dot Technique)

Although the relation between mind and eyes is not very well understood to this day, Dr Bates came up with some astounding insights of rar-reaching practical implication.

He discovered, for example, that by imagining a black dot we can learn to improve our vision, our memory, our imagination, our mental focus and our inner balance at the same time. At first sight this technique seems ridiculously simple, but it is in fact quite involved and requires some training.

In some ways it reminds us of the 'one-pointed thinking' that is described as an achievement of the highest order in certain Oriental scriptures. It teaches us to think of one thing at a time with undivided attention, while letting the mind move freely according to the needs of each moment. It shows us how to avoid the common habit of dividing the attention between two or more things at any given time, which always throws the mind out of focus and makes the world look vague, colourless and confusing. At the same time it shows us how to avoid staring and 'fixing the gaze'.

What has long ago been described in mystical terms as one of the great secrets of the ages, is confirmed in concrete and practical terms by the black dot technique. But whereas the Oriental techniques for reaching the one-pointed state require years of rigorous practice in solitude under the guidance of a teacher, the black dot technique can be learned from this book in a matter of weeks.

You can demonstrate the connection between memory, imagination and vision through this simple experiment: Focus on the full stop at the end of the last paragraph, after the word 'weeks'. Notice how black it is. Let your eyes scan inside and around it for a second or two, then close them and remember the dot. As soon as you picture a really black dot in your mind, your eyes are co-ordinating perfectly and effortlessly. If you now open the eyes and look at the letters around the full stop you can see them much more clearly than before. Repeat this a few times and note how your vision improves as your memory of the black dot improves. The blacker you picture the dot in your mind, the better becomes your eyesight – and the better becomes your memory in general.

As you know from experience, the mind cannot be forced to remember a name or a word or anything else. The memory works best spontaneously, without conscious strain. In this state it also produces more relevant information, the things that really interest and concern you. Of the billions of items stored in your brain it selects with uncanny accuracy the ones that relate to your present desires and needs, the ones that you can use right now. If your mind and vision are out of focus, on the other hand, your memory gets confused and produces all kinds of useless and negative information.

A good example of this is the mental patient on the psychiatrist's couch, who is asked to remember anything and everything about his/her remote past. The bits and pieces that emerge are typically negative and useless, and they serve only to confirm the patient's confused concepts of life. To reconstruct a person's past from these distorted and largely fictitious tales would be difficult if not impossible.* Instead of dwelling on such confusing images of the past, the patient might do better to bring the mind into focus first, which can often be achieved through vision training. Then he/she would see the more meaningful aspects of the past and remember those items that are useful here and now.

The 'black dot exercise' can be practised anywhere and at any time, and after a while you will be able to do it without looking at a full stop on a printed page. At first you may get best results by memorizing the black dot while covering the eyes in the palming position, which excludes all light from your vision and has a relaxing effect. Your eyesight will be sharpest when you imagine a very small

---

*Even S. Freud admitted this in his later works.

73

black dot, but you may find it relaxing to use larger dots and other black items now and then, such as the ones on the next page.

Some people get fairly good results also with coloured objects that produce pleasant mental associations, such as flowers. But the advantage of black objects is that they are uniformly coloured so that the eye does not dwell on any detail. For all practical purposes it is therefore best to avoid any objects that are not completely and uniformly black.

The better your vision, the longer you can remember a black dot. Perfectly functioning eyes may retain the image of a perfectly black dot for many minutes. Eyes in poor condition see the dots and letters on a printed page as more or less grey, they also remember them as grey, and they remember them for a shorter time. If one of your eyes sees better than the other, the better one will see a dot blacker and remember it longer and blacker. You can easily confirm this by closing first one eye and then the other. If you find a difference, it may be advisable to give the weaker eye extra exercise by closing the other one periodically.

In the beginning it will be best if you look at the dot from a distance where you can see it sharpest and where it is well lit. This may be a few inches if you are short-sighted or several feet if you are far-sighted. As your vision improves your range of clear vision will expand and you will also become less dependent on perfect lighting conditions.

After some practice you will be able to recall the mental image of a perfect black dot without first looking at an actual dot. Later you will succeed in visualizing the dot even when your eyes are open. This will enable you to focus sharply on any object in front of you. You can try this out by looking at the following page with the dots and letters. Look at a small dot on the page until it registers completely black, until your eyes are well focused and relaxed. Now retain this image and slowly direct your eyes at one of the letters, so that the black dot merges with the black of the letter. All the dots and letters on the page will suddenly stand out sharper and blacker than before.

As you develop the ability to remember and visualize

the small black dot during your daily activities, you will also notice a feeling of inner balance and centreing. Perfect mental and visual control means that you are more in control of your life and that 'everything is under control', in an easy and effortless way. Your mind/body functions with optimum efficiency, and you can instantly remember a dot or anything else that relates to your present needs. As long as you have to grope for the mental image of the dot for several seconds before it stands out clearly, your memory is not yet perfect and the dot will not come out perfectly black.

At this stage you are probably still a beginner in the art of seeing black dots. Find out where you stand and enter the result in the Black Dot Programme Chart in back of the book. Focus on the full stop at the end of the previous sentence for a few seconds, start palming and see how many seconds the full stop remains black and sharp in your memory. (But don't strain!).

After you have practiced with the black dot technique until you feel comfortable and successful with it, you can extend the basic principle of it to all kinds of everyday objects. Just remember that your eyes see most clearly those objects that seem pleasant and familiar. It is your mind that attaches meaning and significance to the things you see. Your retina may record an optical pattern, but your brain interprets this pattern. To see something really well you have to have a clear mental concept of it. This is why sailors are good at recognizing ships, and why biologists can spot bacteria under the microscope where others see only a tangle of meaningless shapes.

Seeing the Centre Best

If your vision is perfect, you see the centre of your field of vision clearest. When looking at a letter on this page, for example, you see this letter more clearly than the other letters around it. When looking closely at one corner of this one letter, the corner stands out more clearly than the rest of the letter. This is because your retinas are most sensitive in one tiny spot called the fovea centralis. The fovea centralis, which literally means 'central pit', is in turn most sensitive in its very centre, where thousands of light-sensitive cones are crowded into the space of less than a square millimeter. All other parts of the eye are less sensitive in proportion to their distance from this spot. (See illustration on page 28 in How Your Eyes Function). People with normal vision focus the eyes in such a way that the image of the object they want to see at any given time falls exactly on the fovea centralis, so that they see that object clearest. People with abnormal vision, on the other hand, aim the eyes at one object but see another object near to it more clearly. This is called eccentric fixation, which Dr Bates found to be an invariable symptom of all abnormal conditions of the eyes, both functional and organic.

To find out how central your fixation is at present, look at the EYE–Q Chart, first from a distance of one foot, and then of twenty feet. Focus on a letter on the top line and observe if another letter near to it appears sharper or blacker. If not, move on to lower lines and repeat the experiment, until your eyes show the first sign of eccentric fixation. Enter the details in the Centralizing Progress Chart in back of the book, and check again periodically in the coming weeks and months.

Another way of finding out your degree of central fixation is to watch the stars on a dark night. Focus on a barely visible star, then shift your eyes slightly to one side or to another star right next to it. Can you now see the first star better? If so, your fixation is eccentric. Many textbooks claim that this is normal, and that all people see better at night when they aim the eyes slightly away from the object they want to see. This is true enough in view of the fact that most adults nowadays have imperfect vision, and that therefore their eyesight must be more or less eccentric. But the few people who do have perfect vision see that star best at which they are looking.

The mere awareness of this fact can help you to improve your vision, because it implies that the eyes must shift continuously to see anything well, so that the image falls precisely on the fovea centralis. This requires an ability of the mind to concentrate on one thing at a time, without straining. Most people acquire these abilities before school age, but later get into the habit of scattering their attention and looking at things in which they are not really interested, especially in school. To drop this habit requires no great effort, fortunately. On the contrary, it can be unlearned just by relaxing. All optical defects, eccentric fixation and inefficient mental habits are accompanied by strain, and they disappear with the strain.

When you see with central fixation, your vision is perfect, your eyes function effortlessly and can be used almost indefinitely without fatigue. The muscles around the eyes, face and neck are at rest and balanced, and the whole body relaxes. Wrinkles and dark circles around the eyes disappear in time as the habit becomes permanent.

Try this exercise: Put the EYE-Q Card down in front of you where you can see it well. Take your glasses off. Sit in a relaxed position and palm for a minute. Rotate your head several times to relax your neck muscles. Now look at a letter on the lowest line you can read, and also at the other letters around it. Can you see it best when you are looking straight at it, or do you see it best when you focus on another letter near it? Start with the last letter of a long word and shift your eyes gradually to the left, from one letter to the next, through all the letters. At which point did you see the letter best? Now relax once more, rotate your head a few times,

78

palm for at least ten minutes and visualize pleasant scenes in motion. Open your eyes, look at the letter first and then shift to the left again, from one letter to the next. At which point do you see the letter best this time? With continued daily practice the two letters will come closer together as your fixation becomes more central.

Later you will reach a stage when you can look at the letter and see the one next to it less clearly. Finally you will be able to look at the top of the letter and see the bottom less clearly. You will then notice that the whole letter appears black and distinct, because your vision is now nearly perfect, if perhaps only for a fraction of a second at first. But with continued practice the habit of central fixation becomes permanent. After you have become able to see the letter clearly in this way, you can graduate to smaller letters on the EYE-Q Chart. When you can look at the top of a letter in the lowest line and see the bottom of the letter less clearly, you will know that your vision is perfect. Most likely you will then experience a feeling of great relief spreading through your whole mind/body, because some of the accumulated tension of years or decades will suddenly dissolve.

This new harmony in the mind/body has beneficial effects on all parts of it, of course, and many seemingly un-connected organic conditions may gradually disappear as central fixation becomes habitual. Dr Bates noticed to his surprise that even conditions of glaucoma, incipient cata-ract and inflammation of the iris or cornea could be elimi-nated through central fixation. Conditions in other parts of the body were relieved in many instances. He found that all the other senses of touch, taste, hearing and smell also improved, together with the vital processes of digestion, assimilation and elimination. Finally, and not surprisingly, he observed that the efficiency of the mind can be enor-mously increased.

To improve your central fixation, read the fine print on the EYE-Q Chart daily, or use one of the old books that are printed in a small type face. Reading this fine type is espe-cially beneficial in dim light, but make sure your eyes and mind are relaxed when you do this.

Breathing Habits

You can go without food for up to one month, and without water for a week. But without air you can live only about three minutes. Your brain absolutely needs a steady supply of oxygen. Your eyes are extensions of your brain. The body and the nervous system are also dependent on oxygen, of course.

When you are active outdoors, breathing comes naturally. Especially when you walk in natural surroundings, you breathe deeply and rhythmically, and you get a sense of well-being from this. But chances are that you spend much of your time indoors or in man-made surroundings, and that the exercise you get is not very balanced or wholesome.

In addition, we tend to hold the breath when paying close attention to something. This is probably an instinctive reflex that makes us suppress noise and movement, so that we can see and hear better. After the need to pay attention is past, we breathe a sigh of relief or, if we had felt somewhat upset, we exhale convulsively in the form of laughter. In today's world we spend much time sitting indoors, passively reading, watching or listening, and we tend to develop shallow and erratic breathing habits. We hardly ever use our lungs to full capacity, and we get short of breath at the slightest exertion.

Are you normally getting enough air to insure the proper functioning of your mind-body? To find out, take a watch with a second-hand and count how many times you exhale in one minute. Sit in a comfortable position and breathe naturally as you normally would. Start counting when you *ex*hale the next time, and count how many times you *ex*hale until the second-hand has made one full circle. Enter this figure in the Breathing Progress Chart (page 120) in back of the book and check again periodically in the coming weeks.

A person's breathing rate varies also according to age, sex and lung capacity. With most adults it may fluctuate around fifteen breaths per minute (BPM) while sitting, but it should be lower. A rate of 8 BPM is more desirable, and 4 BPM would be ideal for most adults. The slower your breath, the deeper it becomes. Lung capacity decreases with age when the lungs are habitually underused or do not get periodic vigorous exercise.

Next to the quantity of air you inhale you should consider the quality. If you are forced to live in an area where the air is often polluted, be at least sure to keep the air around you as pure as possible. Circulate fresh air into the rooms where you live and work, avoid the smoke exhaled by others, and try to quit smoking if you are a smoker yourself. Try to live near forests, parks, or other areas covered with plant life that purify the air and create oxygen. Pure air is also found near large bodies of water and around mountains.

For thousands of years, the Yogis of India have known that shallow breathing opens the door to all kinds of physical, nervous and mental disorders. They especially warn against the habit of breathing through the mouth (except in emergencies). Breathing exercises form, therefore, the core of Hatha Yoga,* together with exercises that keep the spine flexible. The basic Yoga breathing technique is called Pranayama, and it requires only about five minutes daily: Sit comfortably with eyes closed, with erect spine and feet close to the body or underneath it. Exhale slowly through the right nostril by closing the left nostril with your right middle finger, until the lungs are empty. (Keep a handkerchief handy in case either nostril is blocked). Now wait until you inhale spontaneously, until the next breath comes by itself. Let the air rush in. The moment your lungs are full again, exhale through the left nostril and close the right one with your right thumb. Then repeat this cycle for about five minutes. Change from one nostril to the other

---

The term Hatha Yoga means literally 'Joining sun and moon' or, as we would say, integrating the conscious and unconscious, body and mind, spirit and matter, Yin and Yang.

only when your lungs are full. This sounds complicated, but after practising for a few minutes you will do it automatically. You will then soon notice how this simple exercise gets you into the habit of breathing rhythmically and deeply, while it gives you at the same time a feeling of profound well-being. After some time you will look forward every day to this pleasant ceremony.

You can also improve your breathing while you read this book (or any other). All you have to do is follow a certain pattern while you read each sentence. With this method you actually kill three birds with one stone:

a. You get effortlessly into the habit of breathing more deeply, you get into a good rhythm, and you enjoy a feeling of deep inner rest.

b. You learn to avoid the common tendency toward erratic and superficial breathing while reading. This habit stems, as mentioned above, from our instinct to 'hold our breath' when concentrating on some difficult task.

c. You close your eyes between sentences, which rests them and helps them to function better.

First, find a comfortable seat where you sit fairly erect. A slumping position would impede your breath. Take off your glasses or lenses if you can. Just continue reading the book but exhale slowly with each sentence. Read through the sentence while you keep exhaling. Close your eyes when the sentence ends, and finish exhaling. As you begin inhaling, keep your eyes closed. Open your eyes only after your lungs are filled, when you begin to exhale again. Now read the next sentence while exhaling, and repeat the cycle. Move a finger along the lines to help your eyes find the next sentence. Let your breath come spontaneously and easily. Take your time with each sentence, even if it is a short one. If you come upon an unusually long sentence, read to a comma only, and continue with the next out-breath.

After a few sentences you will get into an even rhythm. Your breath will become deeper, more spontaneous and regular. Soon you will experience the feeling of profound well-being that always comes from breathing well, and that will continue long after you finish reading. By practising this technique for several weeks, fifteen minutes or more each day, you will improve your breathing habits substantially. Your BPM will decrease and your eyes will function better. Keep it up until your breathing is normal at all times.

Later you can begin to practice this way with the book moved slightly out of range, so that your eyes can learn to adjust. If you are far-sighted, move the book a little closer. If you are short-sighted, move it an inch or two farther away. But avoid strain at all times, and never inhale actively. Taking the breath in consciously and intentionally is a sign of an over-anxious attitude toward life. You may consciously exhale now and then to get into a deeper rhythm, however. Note how laughter makes you exhale while fear makes you inhale.

In ecological terms, exhaling is essential not only for you but also for the plant life around you. All plants and trees need the carbondioxide exhaled by animals and humans, and in turn they produce the oxygen we need. If you think more in terms of giving and less in terms of getting, you liberate yourself from the competitive 'grabbing' attitude that makes many people over-anxious today.

A person's vitality becomes apparent in his/her breathing habits. The breath should originate from the bottom of the lungs, near the body's gravity centre in the belly. Nervous people breathe from the middle of the chest. People who have lost touch with life and themselves breathe in short gasps from the shoulders, with tense neck and face muscles. Their thoughts and actions become nervous and top-heavy, and their eyes can no longer function properly. Ancient Chinese scriptures describe the body's gravity centre as the seat of Chi or cosmic life force. Although Chi can travel to other parts of the body, it is at home in the pelvic area, where it serves as an inexhaustible source of life energy.

As you become more aware of your breathing, you can use the following age-old method to channel your healing powers into ailing parts of your body. Simply picture the affected part clearly in your mind and let a healing current flow through it as you exhale. If your eyes need improvement, for instance, let a wave of warm radiance flow through them. Imagine how they slowly regain their full powers of vision, or how impurities are swept out of the lenses. This is best done during palming sessions or while lying in bed, and gives a wonderful feeling of inner harmony. Especially Cataract and Glaucoma can be influenced in this way.

Nutrition

In many cases an improvement of vision has been achieved through diet alone, and spectacular results have sometimes been attained through fasting. This is hardly surprising in view of the fact that the diet of most people today is no longer balanced and natural. The human race has survived for millions of years on a fairly simple and natural diet, but within the past hundred years people in the industrialized countries have begun to eat all kinds of refined foods, usually coloured and preserved with chemicals.

The story of 'beri beri' illustrates this. This illness was first observed in China about one hundred years ago, and doctors could not properly diagnose it. People who caught the disease simply became weak and weaker, and this is how the name originated, the word 'beri' meaning weak in Chinese. Most of the affected people lived near rail road lines, and it was suspected that a new type of germ was responsible. After years of investigation the real cause was found: people near the rail roads ate the newly introduced white (polished) rice, while those living in remote areas were still using the traditional brown (unpolished) rice. The new rice polishing machines removed the outer layer (bran) of the grain which contains vital minerals and vitamins. But people thought the new white rice must be superior because it looked cleaner, and merchants found that it had longer shelf life.

The same happened in the Western countries with wheat, rye and other grains, and white bread began to replace the traditional whole grain breads. The effect was not quite as bad here as in China, where the poorer classes ate practically nothing but rice. But the more informed people all over the world are now discovering the importance of avoiding polished grains and/or of eating additional bran. Not only do polished grains deprive the body of essential trace elements, but they also lack the roughage which is needed in the digestive process. They stuff the body full of soft, mushy carbohydrates which tend to clog up the intestines.

Another pernicious addition to our modern diet is white sugar. Only six generations ago sugar was a rare chemical that pharmacies sold by the ounce. Honey was used for sweetening when available. At present the average American consumes almost five ounces of sugar each day, in the form of sweets, soft drinks, cookies, chocolates, sauces, ice cream, etc. Diabetes is one of the illnesses caused by sugar imbalance in the body, and it is often associated with short-sightedness.

An excessive use of animal fats can cause hardening of the arteries, which in turn can impede the blood supply to the eyes. People who are used to a daily diet of bacon and eggs, lots of butter, dishes containing fatty meats, etc. may be courting arteriosclerosis, heart attack and other unpleasant symptoms, including poor vision. Unsaturated vegetable oils, on the other hand, are quite safe.

To eat excessive amounts of meat can have bad effects on the vision, especially for people who lead sedentary lives, which includes most of us. Meat contains valuable protein along with some undesirable toxins which burden the metabolic system. People in the Far East have derived much of their protein from the soya bean for thousands of years, and soya products like tofu, miso and tempeh have found acceptance in health-conscious circles in the West. The soya bean contains all the amino-acids that the body needs, as opposed to other beans, and it is free of the toxins found in meat. It actually contains lecithin and other substances which keep the body, the veins and the eyes flexible.

Today's average consumer has another temptation to deal with: over-abundance of food. Each supermarket offers thousands of tasty and convenient items, and to over-eat becomes an expensive habit for most people. The idea of eating nothing for a day or two is considered outrageous or dangerous, while it would actually cure many a disease. The eyes of some people do not function properly simply because their bodies are continuously overloaded with food of a questionable nature. You can easily find out if this is the case with you by fasting for a few days in a sensible way, and observing any changes in your eyesight. Consult your doctor first if you are ill in any way. Drink as much water or grape juice as you like, to rinse out impurities. After the second day the hunger will disappear and you will feel light and clear-headed. Arrange to stay at home much of the time, and come out of the fast slowly, eating small quantities of bland food at first. Eat slowly and chew well, enjoy each bite, and try to maintain this habit in the coming weeks. Look at the food and think pleasant thoughts. Have a pleasant dinner conversation and avoid arguments at the table. This ties in with the 'one-pointed' state of mind described in the last chapter. Just as the eyes function best when they focus on one thing at a time, so your digestive organs work best when you eat with undivided attention. Although this may be considered a sign of bad manners in 'high society' or in high-pressure societies, you will have the last laugh when you stay healthy and the others don't.

To really enjoy life and to keep your body/mind in top condition you may also have to revise your attitude toward drugs of all kinds, including alcohol, nicotine, caffeine, cola, medicine, hashish, LSD, cocaine, etc. The purpose of drugs has always been to correct an imbalance in the organism, and no drug is meant to be used permanently, except in rare cases of incurable disease. As long as you can 'take or leave' a drug and use it as will to correct an undesirable condition, the effects may be entirely beneficial. But by using any drug regularly and habitually you are interfering with the self-regulating powers of your organism. If you can no longer sleep at night, for example, the reason is not that you need a sleeping pill. You cannot sleep because you are doing something wrong during the day. Did you eat too much before going to bed, did you drink too much coffee, did you fail to solve a problem or are you worried about something? You will find the reason if you look long enough.

Alcohol is said to be a drug against loneliness, but it does not cure loneliness if drinking becomes a habit. If you feel lonely, the answer may be to make yourself more lovable, desirable or interesting, or to become more useful to others. Alcohol, as well as sleeping pills, can make your vision blur, and the same is true of all other drugs if they are used habitually, simply because they replace one imbalance with another. If you think you cannot face another day without marijuana, because the world around you is so wound up, look a little closer and you will find that the tension you hate is partly in yourself, probably even mainly in yourself. The inner tension is bad, but to suppress it habitually with a chemical is worse.

Well, what is there left to eat if you cut out most of the undesirable things? You can still choose from thousands of delicious dishes, believe it or not. Dozens of 'New Age' cookery books are available, and one of them will certainly suit your taste.

There are no miracle diets that will quickly cure this or that eye disease, unfortunately. But a balanced diet can do wonders, especially if your body has been burdened by an unbalanced diet in the past. Your menu should include some of the things that have been found to be especially beneficial for the eyes, such as:
apricots, cottage cheese, soft boiled eggs, prunes, green salad, carrots, cabbage, soya beans, tofu, green peas, liver, fish, spinach, parsley, mint, cheese, fresh milk, oranges, dates, yoghurt, whole grains, wheat germ and bran. Be sure that your diet contains an adequate amount of Vitamin A, which is essential for the eyes and helps especially against night blindness. Persons getting less than 5,000 units often suffer from tiring eyes, sensitivity to light, and other problems. Your intake of Vitamin A will be sufficient if you eat the foods mentioned above regularly. You will have to resort to vitamin supplements only temporarily, during times of stress or when balanced food is unavailable while you are travelling. Excessive use of Vitamin A (over 20,000 units) can cause thinning of hair, sore lips, nose bleeding, etc.[12] But by eating only two ounces of liver and one cup of diced boiled carrots for example, you get

plenty of Vitamin A (about 20,000 units). Mustard greens and turnip greens are equally potent, whereas iceberg lettuce contains practically no Vitamin A at all. Eat vegetables and fruit raw when possible. Don't over-cook.

Generally speaking you have nothing to worry about as long as you stay away from harmful or useless foods, and make sure that your diet is fairly balanced. Beyond that there is no need to count vitamins, minerals or calories every day.

Blood Circulation

The eyes receive a continuous supply of oxygen and nutrients through the blood stream. Through good breathing and eating habits you can make sure that the blood contains all the essential elements, but whether enough blood actually reaches the eyes is another matter. Your heart and veins have to be kept strong and supple, and the circulation has to be stimulated through frequent exercise.

In the industrialized countries today, more people die of heart disease and stroke than from any other disease. A stroke is a narrowing or breaking of blood vessels in the brain. Most often these diseases are caused by deposits of fatty 'plaques' that slowly accumulate on the walls of blood vessels and impede blood circulation. The main ingredient of the plaques is cholesterol. There is nothing wrong with cholesterol in itself, and we actually need a certain amount of it in our diet. But the daily menu of most people contains an over-dose of this fat in the form of butter, egg yolks, fatty meat, etc. Unsaturated vegetable oils, on the other hand, contain no cholesterol at all. People who do heavy physical work in colder climates burn off a great deal of fat and can therefore safely eat more animal fat, but most of us should use it with discretion.

You can find out about your cholesterol level by having your blood analyzed. A level of 150 is desirable, and over 250 you approach the danger zone where you can assume that plaques are gradually accumulating in your blood vessels. In Japan, where people adhere to a fairly lean diet consisting of fish, seaweed, rice, soy products, etc., the average cholesterol level is around 150, while in the USA it is closer to 250. By eating less animal fat and more fish and soy products you can get out of the danger zone in a matter of weeks. But to dissolve the already existing plaques usually takes years. A balanced way of life with some daily exercises is then the answer.

Certain exercises are especially devised for the benefit of the eyes. The shoulder stand, for example, is one of the best ways to increase blood circulation in the eyes and the brain, while at the same time stimulating the neck. Standing on the head would be even more logical for this purpose, but it involves certain risks; inexperienced people can injure their necks, lose their balance and fall on hard objects, or create excessive blood pressure in the brain by over-doing it. For all practical purposes the shoulder stand brings you all the benefits without the risks, but you should start slowly until you get used to it. One minute at a time will be enough in the beginning. After some weeks you will feel comfortable in this position for several minutes, but to do it longer than that is neither necessary nor advisable. Move the feet up and down in a cycling motion.

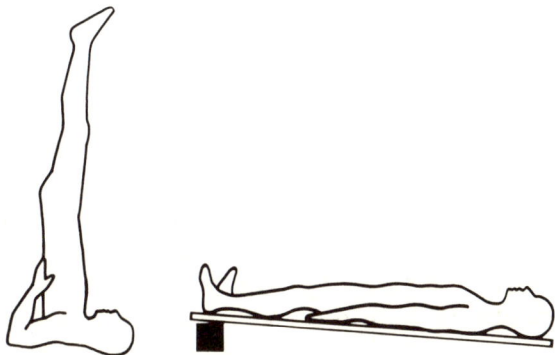

If you do not like the shoulder stand for one reason or another, a slanting board is a good substitute. Lie on it with the head lower than the feet by about eighteen inches, and to stay in this position is quite safe for up to half an hour, if you are in good health. Both the slant board and the shoulder stand can do wonders not only for your eyes, but also for your brain and your hair growth. To make these positions even more beneficial, move the eyes in circles, triangles, squares, infinity signs, etc., as described in Keeping Flexible (page 67).

You can also increase the circulation around the eyes by crouching and touching the floor with your forehead. To make this even more effective, place a bowl with cool, pure water under your head and submerge the eyes and forehead in it. Then roll your eyes and blink under water for a few minutes. Do the same whenever you go swimming. Every morning, when you wash your face, splash cool water gently against your (open) eyes, about twenty times. This will also give the skin of your face a smoother and healthier look. Close the eyelids tightly and open them a few times to exercise the muscles around the eyes.

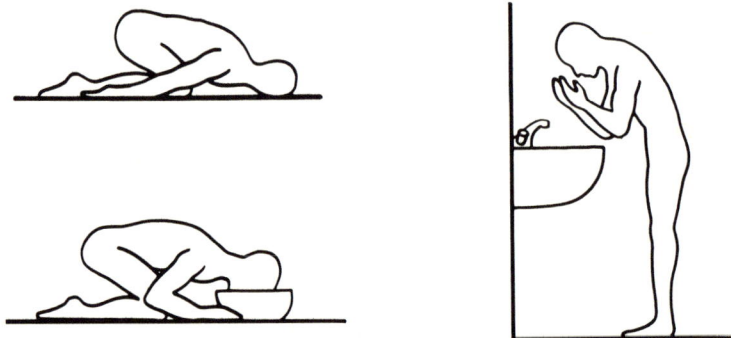

The blood enters your head through the neck, and this can become a 'bottle-neck' when continuous muscular tension and bad posture inhibit circulation. Especially if you lead a sedentary life you should let the neck relax, perhaps every half hour, and move the head in a wide circle a few times. If your posture makes your neck habitually tight, you might want to consult a chiropractor. As mentioned above, such treatment can have an immediate effect on your vision.

While sunlight stimulates blood circulation, nicotine certainly inhibits it, by constricting the blood vessels. If you are a smoker, chewer or snuffer and plan to remain one, your chances of attaining perfect eyesight are limited.

As mentioned above, a diet rich in animal fats tends to clog up the veins. But humans, being part of the animal kingdom, can also produce their own unsaturated fats if they take in too many calories. If you eat too much, your body automatically converts the excess calories gained from foods like sugar, bread, potatoes, ice cream, and even alcohol, into 'animal fat'. To burn up this fat through exercising is practically impossible. To use up the energy contained in one 3 oz. chocolate bar, for example, you would have to jog for one hour. You simply have to reduce your food intake if you want to be slim.

To keep your cardio-vascular system (heart and blood vessels) in shape, you need more than a daily walk around the block. Research has shown that at least twelve minutes of vigorous exercising is needed per day, through activities like swimming, dancing, running, fast cycling or playing a fast game of ball. Slow games like frisbee, base ball or cricket do not qualify.

Your heart rate can tell you if you are in good shape. Count your heart beats per minute first while sitting. The normal rate with men lies between 72 and 76, with women between 75 and 80. Now do some running or skipping for five minutes and count your rate immediately afterward. It should be around 20 beats in ten seconds (120 per minute). If you count again half a minute later, the rate should have dropped to about 15 beats in ten seconds (90 per minute). After another half minute the rate should be back to normal. The longer your recovery time, the more do you need to exercise to get your cardio-vascular system back in condition. Use the Heart Rate Progress Chart in back of the book to monitor your progress periodically.

As a Result you Look Better

What makes a person attractive and good looking? To a great extent, good looks are simply a matter of good health and vitality. Pure complexion and full, shiny hair are considered pre-requisites for female beauty. Another factor is certainly a person's facial expression, especially around the eyes. People with friendly, bright eyes are more attractive than people with hostile or blank eyes.

It so happens that the Bates Method brings out vitality and a bright-eyed, harmonious attitude in people. As the eyes become mobile and relaxed through the exercises described in this book, the whole mind/body functions more joyously.

When you learn the art of seeing, you radiate health and inner harmony to a greater extent than before. You are more at ease with human nature, and with your own nature in particular. The lines and wrinkles of disappointment and worry disappear from your face. You move about with more poise because your movements originate from your gravity centre, and you appear more 'centred' mentally and physically. Your spine becomes more erect and flexible, and your head no longer stretches forward. Your eyes seem steady but lively, they are not 'shifty' and neither do they stare. When speaking to others you maintain continuous eye contact without staring at them. You feel better and you make others fell better.

Although you take good care of your body and you present a well-kempt appearance, you have no desperate need for cosmetics and the latest fashion. You accept your body as it is, with all its strong and weak points.

A famous cosmetic surgeon, Dr Maxwell Maltz, found that many of the people who came to him for cosmetic surgery unconsciously wanted a new personality. After the operation they saw themselves in the mirror but still rejected the image because it reflected the old personality.[13] People who have a poor self-image do not like themselves, and they are not especially liked by others. Through the Bates Method they can learn to see the world and themselves in a more relaxed and realistic way, without distorted expectations.

Although the optical industry tries to convince us that glasses are glamourous, and that every self-respecting person should buy a pair or two, we know deep down that people look better and healthier without them. Glasses not only have a disfiguring effect, but they also create mental discomfort and facial tension.

Almost everything you do to improve your eyesight also improves your appearance. An obvious example is your nutrition (see Nutrition page 85). A balanced diet keeps you fit and slim, it keeps your skin and hair healthy, and reduces tooth decay and body odour. Improved breathing habits and blood circulation contribute further to maintaining a healthy and attractive body, as explained in Breathing Habits page 80 and Blood Circulation page 90. The exercises designed to keep you flexible (page 67) improve your muscle tone and co-ordination, so that your movements become more harmonious or graceful.

The bad effect of nicotine, alcohol and other drugs on a person's skin, smell and appearance is well known. Excessive consumption of animal fat and overly refined foods likewise tends to make the skin leathery, wrinkled or pimply.

Finally, it is a fact that people feel attracted to those who enjoy life and do interesting things. Nothing is as boring as a bored person. Boredom also happens to be bad for the eyes. The eyes function best when they are focused on worthwhile and enjoyable things. The methods described in this book help people to become more interesting by becoming more interested in life.

Your Vision of Life

You can teach the eyes to see better, and at the same time you can learn from your eyes to think better. Because the eyes are really part of your brain, they function best when your mind is well-balanced and finely-tuned, when you have the proper perspective and the right attitude toward life. By improving your eyesight you can improve your vision of life. From what has been said in this book so far you can draw the following conclusions:

Don't force your mind to focus on things that do not really interest and concern you deep down. Your vision blurs and your mind loses its focus as soon as you are bored. Your heart will tell you which things are important in your life at present. Everybody has his/her own ideals and needs. Your ideas of social life, work, hobbies and recreation may differ from those of the people around you. If you feel that a best-seller does not add to your life, put it aside and do something more worthwhile. If certain social circles bore you, make friends elsewhere. If your work bores you, cultivate your interest in another occupational field that fascinates you and make the switch when circumstances allow. Shape your surroundings to suit your sense of beauty, so that you will enjoy looking at them.

Have faith in nature. Encourage the self-curing and self-regulating forces in your mind/body. Use medicines, aids, crutches and glasses with discretion. Long before our present technological age, in 1850, Emerson said: "The civilized man has built a coach, but has lost the use of his feet. He is supported on crutches, but lacks so much support of muscle."[14] By maintaining a healthy balance between mind and body, head and heart, activity and rest, work and play, you can normally avoid illness and the need for artificial aids. If you do become ill, create the conditions that allow the self-recuperating forces to take effect, instead of manipulating the symptoms on the surface.

Keep your mind and eyes mobile. Your mind works best when it is engaged in a continuous process of comparing, evaluating, judging – just as your eyes see best when they scan over and around the thing you are looking at in a continuous motion. A stagnating mind cannot think clearly – just as staring eyes cannot see clearly. "Everything moves", said Heraklitus, and your mind is no exception. Even if a thing seems to stand still, the time passes and with it your perception. Life is not a static condition but a dynamic process, an adventure full of challenges and possibilities.

Don't develop the habit of straining your mind and eyes. Your mind is more complex than the latest and largest computer, and the eyes are an extension of the mind. The team work performed by the billions of cells in the brain is beyond human comprehension, and it requires fine-tuning of the highest order. This is why the mind is most efficient and successful when it functions easily and effort-lessly. A strained mind works clumsily, with much inner friction and with a tendency to provoke conflicts and accidents. You can improve your mental powers by improving your vision, and vice versa.

Learn to focus on one thing at a time. Your mind works best when the attention is aimed sharply at the item that interests you most at any given time. If you divide your attention your mind gets confused and inefficient – just as your eyes begin to blur and hurt when you try to look at two things at the same time. Form a clear mental concept of the thing that occupies your mind at any given time, so that it stands out alive, in three dimensions and colour.

Have a clear idea also of the truth as you see it, without disregarding other people's concept of what is true. Dr Bates found that lying is bad for the eyes because it creates a strain in the mind between truth and untruth. If someone lives knowingly by a double standard or becomes a hypocrite in other ways, the mind/body suffers, together with the vision. The same happens when someone's life lacks focus or unity, or when life and the cosmic order are perceived as meaningless or senseless. Albert Einstein said in this context: "The man who regards his own life and that of his fellow creatures as meaningless is not merely unhappy but hardly fit for life."[15]

Pursue an enjoyable goal. A sense of purpose helps you to think and see clearly, especially if the goal is worthwhile and enjoyable. It creates a sense of dynamic well-being, which makes useless or negative thoughts disappear. The mind/body then functions more efficiently and with less effort, and can more easily deal with external challenges. French sociologist Emile Dürkheim said: ". . . an organism pleased with things injurious to it evidently could not exist. It can then be accepted as a very general truth that pleasure is not linked to harmful states; which is to say that, in the large, happiness coincides with a healthy state."[16]

Part Three

Dealing with Each Visual Defect

What to Expect from the Method

What has been said in previous chapters applies more or less to all types of visual defect. By applying the knowledge and exercises described you create a sound basis for improvement. Through palming, sunning, swinging, the Black Dot Technique and centralizing you help the eyes to function better, which also tends to improve their organic condition in time. By improving your nutrition, blood circulation, flexibility, your breathing habits and the ability to relax you are also bound to help your eyes. This does not mean that you should avoid medical advice and periodic eye examinations, especially later in life or when you feel that there might be something wrong.

The following chapters describe three categories of visual defects, and suggested ways of dealing with them:
Optical defects such as short-sightedness, long-sightedness, presbyopia, astigmatism and squint. These are the most common disorders, constituting about ninety per cent of all cases.
Eye Diseases like cataract and glaucoma.
External problems like conjunctivitis, keratitis and sties.

To what extent can the methods described in this book improve a particular visual defect? The answer depends on many factors. Some disorders are cured almost instantly and completely while others do not respond very well, depending on the person's mental and physical condition, motivation, dedication, living habits, faith in the body's self-curing powers, and depending on how long the disorder has already existed. Serious organic diseases like cataract, for example, have been cured by the methods described here after eminent eye specialists had given up hope – while simple functional disorders like myopia can by psycho-somatic and difficult to correct. The line between functional and organic disorders is often vague, because improved functioning can favourably influence an organic condition and vice versa. The millions of living cells that constitute the eye are continuously renewing themselves, and they respond to the needs of the organism. The more a person needs and really desires to see, the greater is the chance of improvement. Defects are seldom inherited, although a particular inherent predisposition may have to be counter-balanced by appropriate measures.

Short-sightedness (Near-sightedness, Myopia)

This disorder is more common in childhood, and it often recedes again around the age of twenty. The short-sighted person can see near objects quite well but far objects seem blurred, because the eyes cannot adjust to distances beyond a few feet. Contributing factors are the tension and stresses of growing up in a high-pressure society. Nutrition can also be a factor, especially through the preference of children for soft drinks and sweets over wholesome foods. In the poor countries of the third world, where most people do not even go to school, they can become myopic from malnutrition. Children in the richer countries can suffer from malnutrition too if they derive their energy from 'junk foods' for years.

A somewhat limited mental outlook and a fear of distant future developments or responsibilities can also contribute to short-sightedness. The typical myope is physically and mentally somewhat shy and introverted, and he/she can benefit especially from the relaxing exercises and from changing the focus frequently. Sunning, palming, and the seeing or imagining of objects that move from the near distance into the far distance help to relax the tense preoccupation with near objects.

To balance these tendencies you can learn to cut out useless foods from your diet, to cultivate a wider mental horizon, and to relax mentally and physically as you go through the day. At work or while reading at home you can frequently look up and into the distance beyond 15 feet. You can also shift your vision between two identical objects, such as coins and stamps, one of them in your normal reading range and another ten or twenty feet away.

Another simple and effective technique is this: Touch your nose with one finger, then slowly stretch your arm and watch the finger recede. Do this about thirty times a day. Take your glasses off whenever possible, let the eyes learn to accommodate again. At least try to wear a weaker prescription. When reading, put the page slightly farther away to get your eyes used to this distance, without actually straining them. Place one copy of the EYE-Q Chart permanently in a place where you will often see it from a distance, and try to read further and further down the lines, in short relaxed flashes. Relax the neck now and then by rotating the head in wide circles, first in one direction and then in the other. Above all, open your eyes to the wide world and face future challenges.

Far-sightedness (Hyperopia and Presbyopia)

Far-sighted people see better at the distance than close-up, but even their distant vision is limited. Their problems are similar to those of short-sighted persons – but in reverse. The cause lies either in a flattening of the eyeballs or in the hardening of the lenses, but the practical effect is the same in both cases. In the first case we speak of hyperopia or hypermetropia, and in the second case of presbyopia or 'old-sight'. With many people over the age of forty, the lens tends to harden and lose its power of accommodation. This makes presbyopia incurable, according to orthodox theory, and all of us will need glasses as we get older. But countless people over the age of fifty have improved their ability to see at close range through the methods described in this book, which shows that the eyes can learn to accommodate again.

The lens in the eye grows from the inside out over the years, layer by layer, and it is nourished by the aqueous liquid surrounding it. In a poorly functioning organism fewer nutrients reach the inner layers of the lens, and the process of hardening is speeded up. A proper diet can do much to alleviate this problem, together with exercises that increase blood circulation. Certain foods tend to create rigidity in the body while others keep the body supple, as explained in Nutrition page 85. Sunning the eyes and immersing them in cool water will stimulate blood circulation, as mentioned in Resting the Eyes page 55 and Blood Circulation page 90.

But if the lens has lost all power of accommodation, the three pairs of muscles around the eyeball can learn to adjust for close vision by changing the shape of the eyeball. The same type of adjustment is also necessary in the case of hyperopia, when the lens is still functioning but is located too close to the retina.

105

Far-sighted people have difficulty reading at the normal reading distance of 12 – 14 ins, especially if the letters are small or poorly lighted. They can usually be recognized by their habit of holding the page at arm's length to read it. The closer they hold the page, the more blurred and greyish appear the letters.

If you are far-sighted, keep in mind that your vision is keenest at close range when the pupils are as narrow as possible. This is the case when the object is well lit. The same book that you can read very well at noon will become completely illegible at night under a weak light. You may also find that your vision gets blurred by eyestrain towards the end of the day.

Develop your visual and mental mobility, and also read Keeping Flexible (page 67) about the subject of flexibility again. As people get older they tend to settle into rigid habits and attitudes, which can be reflected in their eyes. They also tend to be annoyed by 'silly' details and intricate chores requiring near vision, and they prefer a wide, grand vision of life. They need to realize that quite often 'the little things in life' are the ones that count, and they can learn from children to enjoy small things.

You will find daily exercises with the EYE-Q Chart especially helpful. The letters that appear grey to you now will look more and more black and distinct after practising the Black Dot Technique, mentioned in Visualizing (page 72), for some weeks. Whenever possible, take your glasses off, or at least use a weaker prescription. During your daily activities, make it a point to change the focus frequently, by looking at near and far objects alternately. Move one hand slowly from the tip of your nose to the stretched-arm position and back, and follow it with your eyes, about thirty times. Go out and get a child to play ball or frisbee with you. A frisbee is better because it moves more slowly and can easily be followed by the eyes.

When reading, move the page a little closer to the eyes, without straining them. Close the eyes for a few seconds now and then. Look at a full stop on the page. Let your eyes scan around and inside it, and note how it becomes quite black and sharp.

Above all, remember that poor vision need not be a normal result of growing old. You are as young as you feel, and you can follow the example of the thousands of people who regained their close vision.

Astigmatism

The eyeball is not a perfect sphere but an irregularly shaped organ with transparent layers in front, called conjunctiva, cornea and lens. Like all other organs in the body, these never conform 100 per cent to our idea of perfection. They can also be pulled out of shape temporarily by nervous tension in the muscles surrounding the eyeball, or they can develop a more permanent irregularity that distorts vision.

All eyes are really astigmatic to some degree, but with 'normal' eyes this is not noticeable. Furthermore, the degree of distortion changes constantly, sometimes even from one minute to the next. Today you see the lines in the diagram below in one way, but a week later they may seem to have changed.

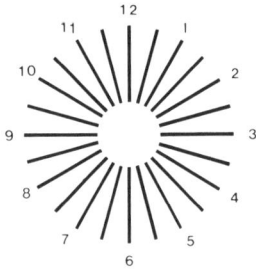

You can detect astigmatism by looking at this diagram. Do any of the lines seem thicker than others? If so, turn the diagram sideways to see if other lines now appear thicker. Close one eye and then the other.

The transparent layers in front of the eye consist of millions of live cells that are constantly renewing themselves and that respond to the needs of the organism. If some of these cells grow irregularly and cause distorted vision, we need not be alarmed. There is a good chance that the eyes will correct themselves if we create the right conditions. By wearing glasses needlessly we would interfere with the natural tendency of the eyes to regulate themselves.

If your vision is distorted, get the eyes into a more relaxed state through sunning and palming every day. Avoid mental confusion, get your life into focus by practising the Black Dot Technique. Let your eyes know that you are concentrating on a worthwhile goal in life, that you will not confuse them with irrelevant distractions. Adopt a balanced diet and a natural way of life.

Squint (Cross-eyed sight, Strabismus)

Normal eyes move in perfect co-ordination, and squinting eyes have lost this ability to some extent, so that each eye looks in a different direction. Even the slightest degree of divergence will impair the vision. The fault lies usually not in the eyes or eye muscles but in the nerve centre of the brain that co-ordinates them. One eye is usually weaker and can be strengthened by covering the stronger one periodically.

The nerve centre can be trained to function normally through the Black Dot Technique described in Visualizing (page 72). As soon as you learn to remember a small black dot (such as a full stop on a printed page), you regain the mental control that is necessary for co-ordinating the eyes. Improvement through this technique can be almost instantaneous in some cases, while in other cases a vision instructor is needed.

Squint is most common in children. Babies up to the age of one year may grow out of it naturally, but after that treatment is advised. This may require much time, dedication and patience. Any impatience would only retard the healing process, and patient as well as teacher should cultivate a completely relaxed attitude. In all cases these efforts should be supported by following the programme described in previous chapters, relating to palming, sunning, central fixation, diet, breathing and keeping flexible.

Cataract

The lens in the eye can lose its transparency and become more and more opaque, often in old age or through diabetes and other disorders of the metabolic system. According to orthodox theory, this is one of the burdens of old age, which can only be cured through operative removal of the lens.

Cataract is not a growth like cancer, however, but a biological change in the tissue. It is greatly affected by a person's diet, living habits and mental attitude. In some cases, a cataract has cleared up through periodic fasting alone, by eliminating toxins from the system, as explained in Resting the Eyes (page 55) and Nutrition (page 85).

Psycho-somatic causes may also contribute, when people 'cannot bear to see an undesirable development'. In such a case the cataract may repeatedly come and go with the event or person that triggers it. The eyes then seem to sense that they are no longer needed or appreciated, and that they may as well turn opaque. All organs tend to atrophy or malfunction sooner or later if they are not used repeatedly and joyfully.

Adelle Davis reports that of the 200,000 Americans who have eye surgery for cataract every year, most are found to have suffered previously from severe stress and inadequate diets.[12]

If you are suffering from cataract to any extent, you should carefully study Part II of the book again, especially with regard to nutrition, breathing, blood circulation, and your vision of life in general. But even if surgery becomes unavoidable and the lens has to be removed, they eye can often learn to see clearly without glasses afterwards, as Dr Bates has shown.

Glaucoma

While normal eyes are only slightly inflated, glaucoma causes excessive pressure inside the eyeballs. It can result in blindness if it is not detected in its early stages. Because it is not painful, people can be unaware of it until some damage has been done to the optic nerve. Later symptoms include a narrowing of the field of vision so that the person sees the world 'through a hole'.

The fact that glaucoma can be induced through over-excitement, drinking excessive amounts of coffee and through general over-exertion suggests that it can often be alleviated by an absence of these things: a balanced way of life without stress, stimulating drugs or spices and over-excitement. Treatment should therefore normally start with the relaxing and sunning techniques explained in Resting the Eyes (page 55) and a balanced diet, together with constant observation by an eye specialist. Exposure to daylight and sunlight often helps to open the drainage channels in the eyes and reduce internal pressure. Adhering to a less liquid diet can also help.

As in the case of cataract (see above), psycho-somatic reasons such as repressed emotions may also play a part, and should be looked into. People can get glaucoma before examinations, by harbouring strong resentments or through fear of confrontation. Resting the Eyes (page 55), Visualizing (page 72), Seeing the Centre Best (page 77) and Your Vision of Life (page 96) deal with these aspects.

Conjunctivitis, Keratitis, Sties

The vision can also be impaired through external eye problems. The outer skin of the visible eyeball (conjunctiva), or the cornea underneath, or the eyelids surrounding it can become infected or inflamed. Although 'germs' or 'dirt' are often blamed for such conditions, the underlying cause lies usually in the weakness or imbalance of the whole organism. By strengthening and detoxifying the body much can be done to make infections disappear, or to prevent them in the first place. The body's own defence system will do its job if it is supported by a wholesome natural diet and proper hygiene. People who suffer from conjunctivitis, sties and acne can usually be identified by their unnatural diet that contains too much sugar, starch and fat, and too little fresh fruit and vegetables.

Conjunctivitis (Pink Eye)

This is an inflammation of the conjunctiva, the thin transparent layer that covers the front of the eyeball and connects it with the eyelids. It can be caused by contagious bacteria, allergies (pollen, cat's hair), or toxins in the environment (chlorine in water, air pollution).

Keratitis

Although the cornea is quite tough, it can be scratched or otherwise damaged, and bacteria can enter. This can lead to serious complications, including permanent opacities or even loss of an eye. After scars heal they can clear in time, especially in younger persons.

Sties

A sty is the infection of one of the small glands around the eyelids, much like acne. An itchy lump appears at first, turns red and later forms a whitish centre filled with pus. The skin finally breaks and the pus is expelled. Sties occur most often in young adults of diminished health. A proper diet can do much to avoid them.

Part Four

Summary and Progress Charts

List of Exercises and Tests

This chapter lists all the exercises, techniques and tests described in previous chapters. Some of them can easily be fitted into your daily routine, while others require extra time. Depending on the type of your complaint, the urgency of your case and the amount of time you have available, you can compose a programme that is tailor-made to your needs. This should also take into account the weakest link in 'your chain of vitality'. You know best where your constitution, your condition or your habits make you particularly vulnerable. You will also sense which of the exercises benefit you more than others, after you have tried them all. Make a list of the ones that you want to do daily. A daily routine will bring faster results than hap-hazard attempts.

The tests and progress charts below have been included as reminders and to make this book more practical. Do not let them make you nervous or over-ambitious. Approach them in a playful, relaxed state of mind. Improvement will probably come in the form of a long-term trend, and temporary delays or setbacks should not discourage you.

If the multitude of tests and exercises confuses you at first, simply select the ones that you can easily fit into your day. Each exercise should be a "mind-expanding" experience that enables you to think and see more clearly in the coming days and weeks. To rush through them merely to get them done would defeat the purpose.

Palming and Sunning (page 55)

Have short or long palming sessions spaced through the day if possible. Picture pleasant scenes in motion, with flying birds, moving clouds, sailing boats etc. Take quick flashes at a letter on the EYE-Q Chart and then see the distinct black image in your mind. During your daily activities, close the eyes now and then for a few seconds. Relax the eyes further by exposing them to the sun or a sun lamp before each palming session, and at other times.

After you have covered the eyes for a minute, do you see coloured spots, or do you see nothing but black?

Date:								
Extent of blackness seen when palming:								

Shifting, Flashing, Blinking
(Keeping the Eyes Mobile page 61)

Shift your eyes quickly from one letter on the EYE-Q Chart to another, until both of them stand out clearly. Shift between small and large letters, near and far charts, and between letters which you picture in your mind. In your daily life, you can shift between any two objects in front of you.

Get into the habit of quickly glancing at objects, at all times during the day. Close the eyes momentarily and remember what you have seen, distinctly and in vivid colour. Objects with sharp outlines in black and white (such as letters) are best.

Keep your eyes and eyelids mobile. Blink frequently in a relaxed and spontaneous way. Take time now and then to do some quick and easy blinking. What is your average blinking frequency at present?

Date:							
Blinks per minute							

118

Keeping Flexible (page 67)

Keep neck and spine flexible through daily exercise. A few minutes of skipping can be done anywhere, even indoors. Move like a willow, not like an oak. Balance your head on top of the spine, do not stretch it forward. Practice the 'elephant swing' that was developed especially to improve the eyes. Use the 'short swing' to relax neck and eyes, also sometimes with eyes closed.

Rotate the neck in a wide circular motion, several times around, in both directions. Bend the head all the way forward, backward and sideways. Roll your eyes in a circular motion, let them describe squares, triangles, letters and numbers. Practise the 'spinal rock' with hands folded around your knees. Then sit on a bed, place the opened book directly behind you and try to see as much of it as possible.

Date:					
How much can you see of the book:					
How far can you rock forward and backward:					

The Black Dot Technique (page 72)

Learn to remember a small black dot or full stop. Picture the dot really black, and retain the image in your mind as long as you can, without strain. Then open the eyes and let the image of the dot merge with an object you want to see. Practise with dots and letters at first, then expand your 'one-pointed' thinking to objects in your everyday environment. Note how this gives you a feeling of inner

119

balance and peace, and how it lets your mind/body function more easily and efficiently.

Date:						
How long can you remember the dot:						

Central Fixation (Seeing the Centre Best page 77)

Follow the complex instructions in this chapter to acquire the habit of central fixation. Look at things with undivided attention, while at the same time letting the eyes move around and over each object in a continuous scanning motion.

Date:			
At which line and in between which letters have you observed eccentric fixation: 1 ft			
20 ft			

Breathing (page 80)

Emphasize *ex*haling, then let the air rush in by itself. Avoid holding the breath when reading or paying close attention to something. Keep the air at home and at work as pure as possible. Breathe through the nose only. Set aside five minutes for the Pranayama exercise every day, before meals. Breathe from the bottom of your lungs, not from your shoulders.

Date:						
Breaths per minute while sitting:						

Nutrition (page 85)

Put emphasis on fresh, natural foods, avoid refined and artificial products. Use whole grain products. Don't over-cook; eat fruits and vegetables raw where possible. Avoid white sugar and products containing it. Eat meat in moderation, be aware of cholesterol in animal fat. Don't over-eat, get by without food for a few days now and then. Eat in a pleasant state of mind and enjoy each bite. Make sure you can 'take or leave' drugs of all kinds, including alcohol, nicotine, caffeine, cola, hashish and sleeping pills. Maintain a healthy balance in your mind/body through a balanced diet.

Blood Circulation (page 90)

Keep your cardio-vascular system in good shape, through exercise and sensible eating habits. Use the shoulder stand or slant board to increase blood circulation in your head and eyes. Each time you wash yourself, splash cool water gently on your open eyes. Better yet, submerge your eyes in a bowl of water for a few minutes. Relax the neck by rotating the head now and then. Expose the closed eyes to the sun or a sun lamp. Get at least twelve minutes of vigor-ous exercise each day. Check your heart rate.

Date:						
Immediately after exertion:						
After 30 seconds:						
After 60 seconds:						

Astigmatism (page 108)

Are your eyeballs distorted today, perhaps through strain

121

around the eyes? Find out by looking at the diagram on page 108.

Date:						
Which line appears thicker:						

Iridology (What Your Eyes Reveal Page 30)

Monitor your state of general health periodically by watching your eyes through a magnifying glass or a magnifying mirror. Are the pupils perfectly round – or are they oval or dented? Are the fibres in the iris dense and evenly arranged – or do you see knots and spaces between them? Any irregularity indicates an imbalance in some part of the body, and may signal an approaching illness that can be prevented.

Date:						
Shape of pupil:						
Condition of fibres:						

Your EYE-Q (page 15)

Test your ability to see at distances of 1 ft. and 20 ft., under good lighting conditions. Also write down any other observations regarding your present state of vision.

Date:						
Hour:						
Near EYE-Q:						
Far EYE-Q:						
Observations:						

Bibliography

1. Laurence Krantz, M.D., in *Healing Currents*, January 1980, P.O. Box 328, Loveland, CO 80537.
2. *Family Medical Guide*, 1965, Meredith Publications, U.S.A.
3. *Encyclopedia Britannica*, 1970, Chicago, U.S.A.
4. Gerard Nierenberg, *How to Read a Person Like a Book*, U.S.A.
5. Bernard Jensen, *The Science and Practice of Iridology*, U.S.A.
6. Eckhard H. Hess, M.D., *The Tell-Tale Eye*, U.S.A.
7. *Adler's Textbook of Ophthalmology*, 1969, W. B. Saunders Co., Philadelphia, U.S.A.
   Sir Stewart Duke-Elder, *Diseases of the Eye*, 1970, Churchill-Livingstone, Edinburgh, Scotland.
8. William H. Bates, *Better Eyesight Without Glasses*, 1974, Holt, Rinehart and Winston, New York.
9. Aldous Huxley, *The Art of Seeing*, 1977, Chatto & Windus, London.
   Harry Benjamin, *Better Sight Without Glasses*, 1979, Thorsons Publications Ltd., Wellingborough, England.
10. John Ott, *Health and Light*, Pocket Books, U.S.A.
11. A. S. Neill, *Summerhill*, Penguin Paperbacks, Harmondsworth, Middlesex.
12. Adelle Davis, *Let's Get Well*, 1965, Harcourt, Brace, Jovanovich, New York.
13. Maxwell Maltz, *Psycho-Cybernetics*, Los Angeles, U.S.A.
14. Ralph Waldo Emerson, *Essays*, 1926, Thomas Y. Crowell Co., New York.
15. Albert Einstein, *Ideas and Opinions*, 1954, Crown Publications, New York.
16. Emile Dürkheim, *Division of Labour in Society*, Macmillan Publications.

Vision Training Institute, 11303 Meadow View Road, El Cajon, CA 92020.
Vision Training Center, 7200 Ventura Blvd. (305), Encino, CA 91316.